D1532233

JUL 1 4 2006

Marijuana

Other books in the History of Drugs series:

Marijuana

EDITED BY JORDAN MCMULLIN

Bruce Glassman, *Vice President*
Bonnie Szumski, *Publisher*
Helen Cothran, *Managing Editor*

GREENHAVEN PRESS
An imprint of Thomson Gale, a part of The Thomson Corporation

THOMSON
GALE

Detroit • New York • San Francisco • San Diego • New Haven, Conn.
Waterville, Maine • London • Munich

For more information, contact
Greenhaven Press
27500 Drake Rd.
Farmington Hills, MI 48331-3535
Or you can visit our Internet site at http://www.gale.com

LIBRARY OF CONGRESS CATALOGING-IN-PUBLICATION DATA

Marijuana / Jordan McMullin, book editor.
    p. cm. — (The history of drugs)
    Includes bibliographical references and index.
    ISBN 0-7377-1957-5 (lib. : alk. paper)
    1. Marijuana—History—Popular works. 2. Marijuana abuse—History—Popular works. I. McMullin, Jordan. II. Series.
    RM666.C266M363 2005
    615'.7827—dc22   2004047474

Printed in the United States of America

CONTENTS

CHAPTER TWO: AMERICA'S INTRODUCTION TO MARIJUANA

CHAPTER THREE: THE MARIJUANA CONTROVERSY IN THE 1960s AND 1970s

of marijuana, public perception of the drug shifted in the 1960s, and people began to question whether the strict laws against marijuana were doing more harm to society than good.

Chapter Four: Current Issues and Debates

Drugs are chemical compounds that affect the functioning of the body and the mind. While the U.S. Food, Drug, and Cosmetic Act defines drugs as substances intended for use in the cure, mitigation, treatment, or prevention of disease, humans have long used drugs for recreational and religious purposes as well as for healing and medicinal purposes. Depending on context, then, the term *drug* provokes various reactions. In recent years, the widespread problem of substance abuse and addiction has often given the word *drug* a negative connotation. Nevertheless, drugs have made possible a revolution in the way modern doctors treat disease. The tension arising from the myriad ways drugs can be used is what makes their history so fascinating. Positioned at the intersection of science, anthropology, religion, therapy, sociology, and cultural studies, the history of drugs offers intriguing insights on medical discovery, cultural conflict, and the bright and dark sides of human innovation and experimentation.

Drugs are commonly grouped in three broad categories: over-the-counter drugs, prescription drugs, and illegal drugs. A historical examination of drugs, however, invites students and interested readers to observe the development of these categories and to see how arbitrary and changeable they can be. A particular drug's status is often the result of social and political forces that may not necessarily reflect its medicinal effects or its potential dangers. Marijuana, for example, is currently classified as an illegal Schedule I substance by the U.S. federal government, defining it as a drug with a high potential for abuse and no currently accepted medical use. Yet in 1850 it was included in the *U.S. Pharmacopoeia* as a medicine, and solutions and tinctures containing cannabis were frequently prescribed for relieving pain and inducing sleep. In the 1930s, after smokable marijuana had gained notoriety as a recreational intoxicant, the Federal Bureau of Narcotics launched a misinformation campaign against the drug, claiming that it commonly induced insanity and murderous violence. While today's medical experts no longer make such claims about marijuana, they continue to disagree about the drug's long-term effects and medicinal potential. Most interestingly, several states have passed medical marijuana initiatives, which allow seriously ill patients compassionate access to the drug under state law—although these patients can still be prosecuted for marijuana use under federal law. Marijuana's illegal status, then, is not as fixed or final as the federal government's current schedule might suggest. Examining marijuana from a historical perspective offers readers the chance to develop a more sophisticated and critically informed view of a controversial and politically charged subject. It also encourages students to learn about aspects of medicine, history, and culture that may receive scant attention in textbooks.

Each book in Greenhaven's The History of Drugs series chronicles a particular substance or group of related drugs—discussing the appearance and earliest use of the drug in initial chapters and more recent and contemporary controversies in later chapters. With the incorporation of both primary and secondary sources written by physicians, anthropologists, psychologists, historians, social analysts, and lawmakers, each anthology provides an engaging panoramic view of its subject. Selections include a variety of readings, including book excerpts, government documents, newspaper editorials, academic articles, and personal narratives. The editors of each volume aim to include accounts of notable incidents, ideas, subcultures, or individuals connected with the drug's history as well as perspectives on the effects, benefits, dangers, and legal status of the drug.

Every volume in the series includes an introductory essay that presents a broad overview of the drug in question. The annotated table of contents and comprehensive index help readers quickly locate material of interest. Each selection is prefaced by a summary of the article that also provides any necessary historical context and biographical information on the author. Several other research aids are also present, including excerpts of supplementary material, a time line of relevant historical events, the U.S. government's current drug schedule, a fact sheet detailing drug effects, and a bibliography of helpful sources.

The Greenhaven Press The History of Drugs series gives readers a unique and informative introduction to an often-ignored facet of scientific and cultural history. The contents of each anthology provide a valuable resource for general readers as well as for students interested in medicine, political science, philosophy, and social studies.

The Power of a Versatile Plant

In his book *The Botany of Desire* Michael Pollan discusses the evolutionary strategies that certain plants have used to survive. He notes that the most successful plants in the world are often the ones deemed most versatile by humans. If a certain plant is believed to be particularly useful—if it can be implemented in people's daily lives in a variety of ways—then humans are more likely to cultivate the plant, and the plant is therefore more likely to thrive. From an evolutionary standpoint, one of the most versatile plants in the world, and therefore one of the most successful, is cannabis (which is the source of hemp, marijuana, and hashish). Throughout history the cannabis plant has appealed to cultures around the world because its many uses have met both human needs *and* human desires. People have used it to make paper, clothing, and medicine and have eaten its nutritious seeds to survive. They have also smoked it as a drug to alter their perception of reality. An examination of some of its uses provides a broad picture of the amazing versatility of the cannabis plant.

The Uses of Hemp

Hemp is a distinct form of the same plant species that produces marijuana: *Cannabis sativa L.* Their leaves look similar but hemp is much taller and more fibrous than the typical cannabis plant. Hemp also only contains trace amounts of THC (delta-9-tetrahydrocannabinol)—the chemical compound responsible for the intoxicating effect of other forms of cannabis. From its stalks, products as varied as clothing, paper, and biodegradable plastics can be made, while its seeds can be used for food, various oils, and fuel.

Hemp has played a role in the development of cultures around the world. Approximately ten thousand years ago the Chinese began experimenting with the hemp plant, and their skill and creativity resulted in textiles, clothing, paper, and foodstuffs made from hemp fiber and hemp seed. With the help of the Scythians—a nomadic, horse-riding tribe that is believed to have originated in the area around the Black Sea— the hemp plant spread throughout the Middle East and Europe. Because it grew well in a variety of climates and because its fibers made such strong, resilient cordage, hemp eventually became an essential part of European trade and exploration; by the middle of the nineteenth century, almost all European ships were rigged with rope made from the cannabis plant.

America's history also was affected by hemp. Thomas Jefferson once claimed that America's future depended upon hemp agriculture, but when the public became aware of and alarmed by the recreational uses of marijuana in the 1920s and 1930s, hemp production in America was outlawed. Although hemp is a different plant than the one that produces marijuana, it was nevertheless lumped into the category of dangerous narcotics. With the passing of the 1937 Marijuana Tax Act, hemp cultivation was prohibited in America. Despite a brief resurgence of prohemp rhetoric during World War II, when the U.S. government encouraged farmers to grow hemp to help clothe soldiers abroad, the cultivation of the cannabis plant, for *any* purpose, is still a federal crime in the United States.

Today the use of hemp is a hotly debated issue. More than thirty industrialized nations grow hemp commercially, including England and Canada. Hemp is legally recognized as a commercial crop by the UN Convention on Narcotic Drugs, the North American Free Trade Agreement (NAFTA), and the General Agreement on Tariffs and Trade (GATT). Products such as clothing and lotions made from imported hemp are experiencing a huge resurgence of popularity in the United States and abroad. Hemp activists around the world claim that if the potential of hemp were fully realized, people would not have to rely on trees for paper or gasoline for fuel. On the other hand, opponents of hemp argue that other resources are just as useful and that the legalization of commercial hemp in America would be the first step toward the legalization of cannabis for recreational purposes.

Cannabis as a Medicine

Certain forms of the cannabis plant, including *Cannabis indica*, contain high amounts of the chemical compound THC. In addition to producing intoxicating effects, this compound alleviates the symptoms and pain associated with chronic illnesses. Even thousands of years ago, cultures all over the world were using marijuana for myriad health problems. The Chinese used cannabis for more than one hundred ailments, including beriberi, constipation, malaria, and even absentmindedness. In India cannabis was used to restore appetite, cure fevers, induce sleep, and relieve various kinds of pain. Until the late nineteenth century, marijuana was held in high esteem by doctors in the West. In the 1840s W.B. O'Shaughnessy, a British physician, praised marijuana as an excellent analgesic, and it is believed that Queen Victoria herself used the drug to relieve her menstrual cramps. Only when people began to speak out against marijuana's potentially detrimental effects on the mind did physicians in the West begin to soften their praise of the drug.

Physicians in the United States had liberally prescribed marijuana throughout the nineteenth century. However, a federal ban in 1937 ended the practice despite some fervent efforts to continue to allow the drug to be used for medicinal purposes. During the congressional hearings conducted before the passage of the Marijuana Tax Act, a representative from the American Medical Association (AMA) insisted that marijuana was known to have some therapeutic applications and that further research should be permitted before the drug was completely outlawed. His testimony, however, was fruitless. The country was so terrified by rumors that marijuana use was rampant in urban areas that Congress was more than willing to pass legislation to crack down on the drug. The use of cannabis for medical purposes is still prohibited by federal law in the United States today. Nevertheless, eight states have passed medical marijuana initiatives that allow patients to use marijuana without being penalized under state law. They can, however, face federal prosecution.

Today the debate over legalizing medical marijuana is contentious. Supporters cite scientific research that shows marijuana's efficacy in relieving the symptoms of many serious illnesses, including glaucoma, multiple sclerosis, Parkinson's disease, AIDS, and even depression. Critics claim that much of the evidence is anecdotal, and that further studies are needed to prove marijuana's medical benefits. Supporters also believe that it is morally wrong for a government to deny patients access to their medicine of choice. Many others, however, argue that it is a greater wrong to allow the sick and disabled to ingest or smoke marijuana because it would set a bad example for children, who might grow up believing that it is acceptable, in certain situations, to use drugs. Some also believe that the battle to legalize medical marijuana is much like the battle to legalize hemp in that both are just steps toward the legalization of recreational marijuana.

In an effort to make medical marijuana more acceptable to the masses, scientists have developed a new, synthetic version of THC that can be taken in pill form: Marinol. Although Marinol offers promise for those who believe in the benefits of THC but do not want to smoke marijuana, many patients claim that the synthetic version is not half as effective as the natural one.

Cannabis the Intoxicant

The fact that cannabis can be used to make thousands of different products and that it can act as a medicine is certainly part of the reason the world remains so enraptured by it. The other part of the story, however, involves rapture itself. When smoked or ingested, cannabis is a mind-altering substance. Users describe feelings of euphoria, giddiness, talkativeness, and tranquility, as well as greater sensory perception. Cannabis thus fulfills what some consider a primary human desire to experience a heightened or altered sense of reality.

People's perceptions of recreational cannabis use and its consequences have changed dramatically throughout history. The Scythians smoked marijuana as early as 400 B.C. as part of their religious rituals. Similarly, the ancient Hindus in India regarded cannabis as a holy plant essential to one's path toward the divine. When Napoléon's military exploits brought him to Egypt in the early nineteenth century, his soldiers were introduced to hashish smoking, which (despite the general's admonitions) they promptly brought back with them to France. For a while, the use of cannabis was associated with artists in Europe, who would gather to partake of hashish and then write about their experiences. In 1930s America, marijuana became associated with poverty-stricken immigrant communities, degenerate youth, and urban crime. Around thirty years later, the drug developed a new association. Instead of viewing marijuana as a drug that incites violence, people began to worry that it caused the youth to become lazy, "drop out" of society, and to lose all motivation to achieve success. Even today people have sharply different opinions about whether cannabis is beneficial or detrimental.

The debate over legalizing the recreational use of marijuana is, not surprisingly, even more contentious that the debates over legalizing hemp production or medical marijuana. In countries where marijuana is illegal, such as the United States, some people argue that the punishment far outweighs the crime—that no worse harm can befall a person from the use of marijuana than arrest and imprisonment by the government. Still, opponents of the drug argue that, even if it has not been proven physically addictive, daily use of marijuana can cause a serious and detrimental psychological dependence—enough to compromise a person's future. In fact, both scientists and laymen debate the physical consequences of cannabis use. While some believe that moderate use has little to no harmful effect on the body, others argue that it contains cancer-causing agents and that marijuana alters the basic function of human cells. Although the full truth about the consequences of marijuana use is still unclear, it probably resides somewhere between the two extremes. As long as the legalization of marijuana continues to be a debated issue, more information will certainly come to light.

A Highly Controversial Plant

The remarkable versatility of cannabis has undoubtedly intensified the controversy over its use and legalization. If it were merely a source of a recreational drug, perhaps people would be more willing to write it off as a dangerous substance and agree with the laws banning it. However, its uses extend far beyond intoxication, causing many people to want legal access to the plant. In *The History of Drugs: Marijuana*, the authors explore the history of the uses of the cannabis plant around the world and the many controversies it has provoked.

CHAPTER ONE

Marijuana's Early Years

A Global History of the Hemp Plant

Rowan Robinson

In the following excerpt Rowan Robinson provides evidence that the hemp plant was used for various purposes throughout history. Even twelve thousand years ago, the Chinese used hemp in their clothing, paper products, cooking, and medicine. In India the plant was used for its fiber and consumed for its psychotropic and healing effects. In the Arab world, a branch of Muslims called the Sufi held hashish consumption dear. In Egypt the plant had been used since the third millennium B.C., both as a medicine and as rope to help in building the pyramids. Eventually, with the help of Dutch settlers, Africans across the continent were smoking cannabis from pipes. The Greeks and Romans of ancient Europe used hemp fabric extensively. Throughout medieval Germany and France, peasants included hemp in their folk remedies and agricultural rituals. By the fifteenth century foreign trade and conquest compelled many European countries to increase their cultivation of hemp, because ships rigged with hemp ropes were the most durable. Unable to produce its own hemp and tired of buying it from Russia, England began to focus on growing hemp in its colonies in the New World. Rowan Robinson is the author of *The Hemp Manifesto: 101 Ways That Hemp Can Save Our World* and *The Great Book of Hemp: The Complete Guide to the Environmental, Commercial, and Medicinal Uses of the World's Most Extraordinary Plant*.

Rowan Robinson, *The Great Book of Hemp: The Complete Guide to the Environmental, Commercial, and Medicinal Uses of the World's Most Extraordinary Plant*. Rochester, VT: Park Street Press, 1996. Copyright © 1996 by Park Street Press. All rights reserved. Reproduced by permission.

The history of mankind does not exist in a vacuum. Our story is interwoven with the stories of countless other species, and as we make these wild plants and animals a part of our lives, both our course and theirs change forever. If we are to understand our future, then, we must look to many pasts. By understanding these other stories, we help to explain our own.

No plant has had as complex a relationship with humanity as has hemp. Hemp's remarkable story does more than develop docilely beside our own; instead it weaves back and forth across our trail, disappearing entirely at times, only to reappear when least expected, often from an entirely new angle. It begins, appropriately, back at the beginning.

Hemp in Prehistoric China

Hemp probably evolved in central Asia, where it became the first fiber plant to be cultivated. Cotton from India and Mediterranean flax were not introduced until thousands of years later. At this nascent stage of civilization, hemp was one of the threads that held communities together. Humans had previously tamed crops (including hemp) for food, but hemp gave them material readily available for the crafts they had begun to master. The masses relied on hemp for all their clothing; only the wealthy could afford the luxury of silk. Hemp and mulberry (the food of silkworms) were such important and widespread crops that the phrase "land of mulberry and hemp" was synonymous with China.

An abundance of evidence from burial pits and other sites throughout China demonstrates the continuous cultivation of Asian hemp from prehistoric times. A twelve-thousand-year-old Neolithic site unearthed at Yuan-shan (in what is now Taiwan) included remains of coarse, sandy pottery with hempen cord marks covering the surface, along with an incised, rod-shaped stone beater used to pound hemp. A late Neolithic site (circa 4000 B.C.E.) in Zhejiang province provides evidence of several textile articles made of hemp and silk. . . .

Hemp as Paper

Early books were limited by the bulk and weight of wooden and bamboo tablets and the expense of the rare silken "protopaper" *zhi*. During the Han Dynasty (207 B.C.E.–220 C.E.) it was discovered that the fibers of hemp made an inexpensive and nearly weightless writing surface when pounded together with mulberry bark. The dynastic history *Hou-Han Shu* attributes the invention of paper in 105 C.E. to Marquis Cai Lun, Prefect of the Masters of Techniques during the reign of Emperor He Di. Archaeologists have recovered older specimens of hemp paper from the Western and Eastern Han periods in Xinjiang, Inner Mongolia, and Shaanxi, however, so it is apparent that Cai Lun only supervised the art of papermaking by craftsmen, though he also worked to promote its use in the imperial bureaucracy. According to chapter 108 of the *Hou-Han Shu*, "He submitted the process to the emperor in the first year of [Emperor] Yuan-Hsing [of the T'ang Dynasty] and received praise for his ability. From this time, paper has been in use everywhere.". . .

Hemp paper is pliable, tough, fine, and waterproof and these characteristics made it popular and preferred for use in official documents, books, and calligraphy. The [sacred book] *Hsin Thang Shu* says that the Chin Dynasty court provided the scholars in the Academy of Assembled Worthies with five thousand sheets of hemp paper each month. . . .

Cannabis in India and the Middle East

The Chinese may have been the first people to make use of hemp's fiber, but it was in India that the more lofty qualities of the plant were first fully appreciated. . . . Hemp became such an integral part of the Hindu religion that bhang and [Hindu god] Shiva became inseparable. Indian mythology says that hemp was present with Shiva at the beginning of the world, and, since modern science believes the plant may have originated somewhere around the Himalayas, we have no reason to doubt this.

Even in India hemp was not always used in a religious set-ting. Warriors were known to drink bhang to calm their nerves before battle, and, as everywhere else the plant was cultivated, hemp was used to cure a wide range of ills. . . .

The Aryans who invaded India also penetrated the Middle East and spread into Europe as far west as France, sowing hemp seed wherever they went. But hemp had beaten them to Mesopotamia. One of the oldest archaeological relics in exis-tence is a fragment of hemp cloth found at Çatal Hüyük that dates to about 8000 B.C.E. The plant is mentioned in Assyrian texts, where it is called *qu-nu-bu*, a "drug for grief." Other for-mulas used *qunu-bu* as a stomachic, aphrodisiac, poultice for swelling, and as a fumigant. The Phrygian tribes who invaded the Hittite empire about 1000 B.C.E. also wove with true hemp fiber. Excavation of the Phrygian city of Gordion near Ankara, Turkey, unearthed hempen fabrics produced in the late eighth century B.C.E. Cannabis is mentioned in cuneiform tablets dat-ing from 650 B.C.E. (and these are almost certainly copies of much older texts) that were found in the library of the Baby-lonian emperor Ashurbanipal. . . .

The Hemp Plant in North Africa

By the third millennium B.C.E., the true hemp plant was known in Egypt, where the fibers were used for rope. The ancient Egyptian word for hemp, *smsm t*, occurs in the Pyramid Texts in connection with ropemaking. Pieces of hempen material were found in the tomb of the pharoah Akhenaten (Amenophis IV) at el-Amarna, and pollen on the mummy of Ramses II (circa 1200 B.C.E.) has been identified as cannabis. The Ram-ses III Papyrus (A. 26) offered an opthalmic prescription con-taining *smsm t*, and the Ebers Papyrus gave "a remedy to cool the uterus," an enema, and a poultice to an injured toe-nail, each containing *smsm t*.

Hemp was used in the construction of the pyramids, not only to pull blocks of limestone, but also in the quarries, where the dried fiber was pounded into cracks in the rock, then wetted. As the fiber swelled, the rock broke. . . .

The Punic people who built Carthage in North Africa dominated the Mediterranean Sea from the eleventh to the eighth century B.C.E. and continued as a lesser power until the Romans destroyed them during the three Punic Wars in the third and second centuries B.C.E. A Punic warship found off the coast of Sicily yielded a large quantity of hemp stems; archaeologists speculated that hemp was rationed to the oarsmen, who chewed on it for mild relief from fatigue. Hemp also was used as caulking in ships' hulls, and of course for rope. . . .

The consumption of cannabis for spiritual masons or for pleasure eventually became common throughout Africa.

The Hippies of the Arab World

Hashish was known in all the Arab lands, but among one religious sect, the Sufis, it became a part of the religion itself, much as bhang and ganja had among the Hindus. The Sufis—so named because they wore wool (suf) for penance—diverged from other Moslems in their belief that spiritual enlightenment could not be taught or gleaned through rational perception, but only in states of altered consciousness. One method of achieving this entranced state was by the use of hashish. Because of their hashish use, their ascetic ways, and because they came primarily from the lower classes, the Sufis were ostracized by other Arabs. Still, they had strengthened the connection between hashish and Arab spirituality, a connection that remains to this day.

Early Drug Enforcement

As the hippies of the 1960s were mirrored by the Sufis of the middle ages, so the war on drugs by current world powers has its predecessors in history. Most notorious of these forerunners is Cairo's 125-year crusade to purge itself of hashish. In

1253 the streets of Cairo were filled with Sufis, and consequently filled with hashish. Hemp grew throughout Cafour, a garden in the middle of the city. The authorities decided the situation was out of hand, and every hemp plant in Cafour was destroyed in a huge bonfire that was visible for miles.

As any observer of the modern drug wars could have predicted, this only drove the production of hemp outside the city. Farmers happily supplied Cairo with its hashish until 1324, when once again the government attempted to separate its citizens from their hashish. For thirty days troops were sent into the fields to destroy every hemp plant they could find. But the city soon learned that, while it might be able to control what grew in its gardens, the countryside was too wide and varied and growing hemp was too easy and too lucrative.

In 1378 Cairo took the next step, an ominous one from our perspective: the torture and murder of its citizens. Under orders from Soudan Sheikhoumi, the emir of Joneima, the farmers of *qinnab* were hunted down and executed or imprisoned. The known users were rounded up and had their teeth yanked out with tongs by soldiers before horrified citizens who had assembled nearby. Hashish use continues, of course, to the present day. . . .

Greek and Roman Uses of Hemp

The Scythians carried hemp from Asia through Greece and Russia into Europe, and later Arabs brought hemp from Africa into Spain and other ports of entry on the Mediterranean Sea. Thanks to their love of the nutritious seed, birds also did their unwitting part to spread hemp's global cultivation.

[The Greek historian] Hesychius reported that Thracian women made sheets of hemp. Moschion (circa 200 B.C.E.) left record of the use of hemp ropes by the tyrant Hiero II, who outfitted the flagship *Syracusia* and others of his fleet with rope made from the superior cannabis cultivated in Rhodanus (the Rhone River Valley). Other Greek city-states obtained much of their hemp from Colchis on the Black Sea. . . .

The Roman empire consumed great quantities of hemp fiber, much of which was imported from the Babylonian city of Sura. The cities of Alabanda, Colchis, Cyzicus, Ephesus, and Mylasa also were major centers of hemp industry. Cannabis was not a major crop in early Italy, but the seed was a common food. Carbonized hemp seeds were found in the ruins of Pompeii, buried by the eruption of Mount Vesuvius in the year 79. . . .

The Venetians and the Vikings

The Italians called hemp (or *canappa*) *quello delle cento operazioni*, "substance of a hundred operations," because it required so many processes to prepare the fibers for use. The Venetians eventually came to dominate the Italian hemp industry, instituting a craft union and the Tana, a state-operated spinning factory with demanding production standards. The Venetian senate declared that "the security of our galleys and ships and similarly of our sailors and capital" rests on "the manufacture of cordage in our home of the Tana." Statutes required that all Venetian ships be rigged only with the best quality of hemp rope. From its advantageous location, the superior Venetian fleet controlled Mediterranean shipping until the city was conquered by [French emperor] Napoléon [Bonaparte] in 1797.

The Romans helped spread hemp through Europe, although the plant was well known there already. A sixth-century B.C.E. tomb at Wilmersdorf (Brandenburg) offered up an urn containing sand and an assortment of plant fragments, including hemp seeds and pericarps, when it was excavated by German archaeologist Herman Busse in 1896. The Vikings relied on hemp as rope, sailcloth, caulking, and fishline and nets for their daring voyages; thus, they may have introduced cannabis to the east coast of North America. Hemp seed was found in the remains of Viking ships that must have been built about 850. Equally ancient retting pits have been discovered in Denmark. . . .

Cannabis in Germany and France

Farther to the south, the path of hemp had traveled with the West Germanic people known as Franks, who entered the Roman provinces in 253 C.E. and eventually occupied most of Gaul. When the crypt of the Frankish Queen Arnemunde (who died in 570) was unearthed, she was found surrounded by spectacular treasure and wearing a silk dress and gold jewelry. The body was draped in hemp cloth, showing that the humble plant was held in high esteem.

Hemp figured in the fire festivals of several European countries. In the French Ardennes it was believed vital that the women be intoxicated on the night of the first Sunday in Lent if the hemp were to grow tall that season. In medieval Swabia, in southwest Germany, the nubile men and women leaped hand-in-hand over a bonfire crying "Grow, that the hanf [hemp] may be three ells [equal to 45 inches each] high!" . . .

Hemp in the British Isles

Pieces of hemp rope found in the well of a Roman fort—on the Antonine wall at Bar Hill in Dunbartonshire—indicate that the Romans introduced cannabis to the British Isles at least by 180 C.E. The plant was not cultivated and retted in Britain until about 400, however, when hemp and flax were first grown at Old Buckenham Mere.

The Saxons who occupied Britain about 600 C.E. also cultivated hemp and incorporated it into their medical literature. *The Commonplace Book* (LXIII c., folio 147a) gives a "Rite for Salve, Partly Irish" that contains hemp, placed high on the list of fifty-nine ingredients. . . .

Although the sixteenth-century demonologist Jean Wier warned that hemp caused one to lose one's speech, to laugh without control, and to have magnificent visions, and in the seventeenth century demonologist Giovanni De Ninault named hemp flowers and the oil of hemp seed as principal ingredients of Satanic unguents, peasants continued to believe in the magical power of hemp, and practiced their traditions as ever. On Saint John's Eve, farmers would pick flowers from some of their hemp plants and feed them to their livestock to protect the animals from evil and sickness. Hemp was a common and popular folk remedy, used to treat toothaches, to facilitate childbirth, to reduce convulsions, fevers, inflammations, and swollen joints, and to cure rheumatism and jaundice. . . .

Hemp on the Seas

By the fifteenth century the struggle for power in Western Europe had become a struggle to dominate the seas. Spain, Holland, and England were envious of the riches from the Orient reaching Venice via the silk road, but realized that their location excluded them from the land trade routes. The only way to get a piece of the action was to bypass these routes entirely by establishing a sea trade that led right to their door. This meant they needed hemp, and lots of it—only the long, strong fibers of hemp could produce canvas sails and thick rope tough enough to weather the punishing journey to the Orient. Without hemp, Europe's ships would be stuck hugging its gentle coasts.

The Dutch took an early lead in hemp production because of superior technology and equipment. In Holland, windmills (themselves powered by hemp sails) provided power to crush the stalks of *hennep*, an enormous saving of manual labor that enabled the Dutch to produce vast quantities of *canefas* ("canvas," from the Latin *cannabis*) and rope that aided their ascendance as a powerful seafaring nation. The Dutch used advanced techniques of bleaching hemp and linen; in 1756 they introduced dilute sulphuric acid to the six month process for retting, washing, heating, and watering, and cut the time required in half. Still, Holland faced the same problem as their western rivals: they could not grow nearly enough hemp to meet their needs. The Dutch traded with the Scandinavian and Baltic countries, and especially with Russia and Italy, for their provisions of the strategic material.

Because of their island location, the British were in an even more compromising position than Holland or Spain, since they depended on hemp to maintain their naval power as well as their mercantile interests. As early as 1533, King Henry VIII required all farmers to cultivate one quarter acre of hemp or flax for every sixty acres of land under tillage. Queen Elizabeth repeated the edict in 1563, but farmers were so reluctant to grow the crop that the order was repealed in 1593. With arable soil at a premium, British farmers were not enthusiastic about growing hemp; it did not pay well (even with the incentive of bounties granted by the Crown) and farmers did not know much about the plant's requirements and subtleties. The conservative farmers could not be confident of success with the crop, and most could not afford to experiment. They did not appreciate the labor involved in retting hemp, nor the foul smell. . . .

Looking to the New World

Despite all her efforts, England remained dependent on Russia for as much as 97 percent of her hemp. Not only was this economically crippling, it also placed England in constant jeopardy; all an unfriendly power had to do was cut off her hemp supply, and England would be at their mercy. (Napoléon would later attempt to do just this.) Desperate to safeguard her independence, and having had no luck doing so at home or elsewhere in Europe, England shifted her gaze westward.

For indeed the Atlantic was no longer the beast it had always seemed. Hemp and some intrepid navigators had seen to that. Christopher Columbus had ridden eighty tons of hemp rigging and vast stretches of hemp canvas across the Atlantic in 1492. The Spanish had found poorly defended kingdoms of vast wealth in the new world, and the thought of pillaging a few northern kingdoms appealed to England as well. The *Mayflower*, also powered by hemp, had made the crossing, and reports were that hemp grew beautifully in the new world, better than it ever had in Europe.

And so they came. Hemp's story and mankind's story had twisted together for millennia, but never before had their expansion been so interdependent, and never would anything in their mutual past be as bizarre as the twists and turns that lay ahead. For by beckoning their ships to go farther and faster, and with its natural affinity for the soils and climates of the new world, hemp seemed to almost usher civilization into the next great development on the world stage—that noble, tragic, contradictory experiment called America.

The Uses of Marijuana in India

Garcia da Orta

Garcia da Orta (1501–1568) was a physician in Portugal when he enlisted in the civil service in India in order to satiate his curiosity about the strange new drugs rumored to be there. Written as a dialogue between himself and a colleague named Ruano, *Colloquies on the Simples and Drugs of India* provides a thorough description of all the natural medicines in use in India at the time. The following excerpt is Orta's entry on the hemp plant, which Indians call bhang. Orta reports that bhang can be used to treat insomnia and stimulate the appetite. He also describes the euphoric effect of the drug. He concludes the entry, however, with a warning: Bhang can have unpleasant effects on users if they are unaccustomed to it. First published in 1563, Orta's book caused a stir among European physicians, who were fairly unfamiliar with the medicinal plant. Because of his report, physicians began to look at the hemp plant in a different light, considering its usefulness in new areas of medicine and science. When the Portuguese Inquisition found out after his death that Garcia da Orta was Jewish, they tried to burn all editions of his *Colloquies*. Luckily, a few copies of this watershed document in the history of psychopharmacology were saved.

Ruano

What is the difference between that which they call *Bangue* [the standard spelling is now bhang] and *Amfiam?* It seems to

Garcia da Orta, *Colloquies on the Simples and Drugs of India*, edited by Conde de Dicalho and translated by Sir Clements Markham. London: Henry Sotheran, 1895.

me that they are one, for when you abuse your servants you sometimes call them *Bangue* and sometimes *Amfiam*. I, therefore, wish to know whether there is any difference between the two words.

ORTA

The *Amfiam* we call opium, of which I will speak to you when we come to it. I will now satisfy you respecting the nature of *Bangue*, its tree and seed. Antonia! give me what I told you to bring.

ANTONIA

Here is the tree of the small ones, and see here is the seed, and here is what they sell in the drug shop. For you told me to bring them altogether.

Consumption of Seeds and Leaves

RUANO

This seed is like that of flax (*Alcanave*[1]), except that it is smaller and not so white, and the little tree is also like flax, so we need not discuss them because we already know all about it.

ORTA

It is not flax . . . for the seed is smaller and not white, and the Indians eat either the seeds or the pounded leaves to assist or quiet the women. They also take it for another purpose, to give an appetite; and our writers say that the branches have much inside and little rind, which is contrary to what the flax . . . has.

RUANO

Do they make cords of this bark?

ORTA

No.

RUANO

Is there anything else from which they do make cords?

1. the old Portuguese name for flax, now called canhamo

ORTA

Yes. From the fruit of the palm, which I shall touch upon further on. Also in *Balaguate* they make cords from the roots of a very large tree, and, to confess the truth, they also make them from the flax . . . which is plentiful there, but not in the Deccan or Bengal. I saw there our flax from which we make our shirts, and all this flax is merchandize to be met with in the above countries. They call it alci. But there is very little of the flax . . . on the mainland. What is here is not the flax. . . .

RUANO

Be it so; and now tell me how this *Bangue* is made, and how and for what it is taken.

Pleasant Effects of Bangue

ORTA

They make the pressed leaves, sometimes with the seeds, into a powder. Some inject *Areca verde*, and those who drink it become beside themselves. For the same purpose they mix nutmeg and mace with it, and there is the same effect in drinking it. Others inject cloves, others camphor of Borneo, others amber and *Almisque*, others opium. These are the Moors, who are much addicted to it. The profit from its use is for the man to be beside himself, and to be raised above all cares and anxieties, and it makes some break into a foolish laugh. I hear that many women take it when they want to daily and flirt with men. It is also said, but it may not be true, that the great captains, in ancient times, used to drink it with wine or with opium, that they might rest from their work, be without care, and be able to sleep; for the long vigils of such became a torment to them. The great Sultan Bahadur said to Martin Affonso de Souza, to whom he wished every good thing and to whom he told his secrets, that when, at night, he wanted to go to Portugal, Brazil, Turkey, Arabia, or Persia, he only had to take a little *Bangue*. This was made up into an electuary [confection] with sugar and spices, and was called *Maju*.

Some Unpleasant Effects

RUANO

Has it this pleasant effect on everybody?

ORTA

It may be that it has this effect when we have become ac-
customed to it. I myself saw a Portuguese jester, who was for
a long time with me in Balaguate, eat a slice or two of the electuary, and at night he was pleasantly intoxicated, his utterance
not intelligible. Then he became sad, began to shed tears, and
was plunged in grief. In his case the effect was sadness and
nausea. Those who saw or heard of it were provoked to laughter as if it was an ordinary drinking bout. Those of my servants
who took it, unknown to me, said that it made them so as not
to feel work, to be very happy, and to have a craving for food.
I believe that it is so generally used and by such a number of
people that there is no mystery about it. But I have not tried it,
nor do I wish to do so. Many Portuguese have told me that
they have taken it, and that they experienced the same symptoms, more especially the female partakers. However, this is
not one of our medicines and we had better not waste any
more time over it.

Cannabis in Nineteenth-Century Europe

Carol Sherman and Andrew Smith with Erik Tanner

In the following excerpt Carol Sherman and Andrew Smith describe the popularity of the drug in England and France during the nineteenth century. In the early 1800s marijuana was already used in England to treat a variety of illnesses. When physician W.B. O'Shaughnessy wrote a report in 1839 praising the many medical benefits of marijuana, he attracted the attention of European and North American doctors, who began to prescribe the drug in great numbers. At the same time in France, hashish, the concentrated resin from the flowering tops of the female hemp plant, was becoming popular. In 1840 Jacques-Joseph Moreau founded the Hash-Eaters Club in Paris, where artists and intellectuals gathered to study the effects of hashish on consciousness. By the end of the century, however, marijuana had lost much of its appeal. Doctors began to favor newly developed synthetic drugs over marijuana. In addition, members of hashish clubs in both England and France eventually denounced the drug as dangerous. Carol Sherman and Andrew Smith are the authors (with Erik Tanner) of *Highlights: An Illustrated History of Cannabis*.

Cannabis started off the nineteenth century on a roll. Hemp was a hit in most countries interested in developing their economy through international trade. At the same time, cannabis was beginning to earn a reputation in the West as a powerful, if not an overpowering, drug. Physicians had been aware of the medicinal and mind-bending power of pot since at least 1563, when the Portuguese medic Garcia Da Orta wrote about the drug in his *Colloquies on the Simples and Drugs of India*. Not only did he explore some of the popular medicinal uses for cannabis, but detailed firsthand accounts from drug users themselves, decorating the stories with lurid gossip of horny, cannabis-crazed women and stoned suitors.

The Indian Hemp Tax

On the eve of the nineteenth century, two seemingly unrelated events took place, which together sealed pot's fate for the next one hundred years and laid the groundwork for our modern-day marijuana prohibition. In 1798, the British East India Company went broke; that same year, [French emperor] Napoléon's armies invaded Egypt. The first event was important because it brought cannabis-as-drug to the public eye in Europe. The British Parliament was forced to bail out the once-flourishing company, and in an effort to recoup its losses, the Crown decided to impose a tax, which came to be known as the Indian Hemp Tax, on certain Indian industries, including those involved with the production and refinement of the cannabis-based drugs *bhang*, *ganja*, and *charas*. In the debate that followed, the government defended the tax—a callous attempt to extort money from its impoverished colony—by saying it was in India's best interests. The argument had some support, predominantly from the ruling class. Crime, madness, and social turmoil were everywhere, and *ganja* took the blame.

Why *ganja*? *Bhang* was considered a mild intoxicant, like tea or coffee, and hardly worth worrying about, while the highly refined *charas* was expensive and available only to the wealthiest members of Indian society. *Ganja* was cheap and potent, the drug of choice for India's massive masses. Many Indian leaders wanted the drug banned altogether, but the British scuttled that idea in favor of increased taxes until the cost of the drug became prohibitive. It was a theory, of course, but served its purpose. Undaunted by the tax, Indians kept getting high, as the British tax revenues got higher.

Increased Interest in England and France

Meanwhile, back in England, British doctors were turning to the drug with interest. English physicians stationed in colonial India were the first to hear stories of this wonder drug—the aspirin of its age—which could lower fevers, cure migraines, aid in digestion, induce sleep, even cure venereal disease. By the early 1800s, the drug was popular medicine in England for every imaginable ailment: epilepsy, tetanus, asthma, postpartum depression, rheumatism, gonorrhea. Even Queen Victoria jumped—well, waddled—onto the cannabis bandwagon. In a famous story, her personal physician prescribed cannabis as a treatment for severe menstrual cramps. . . . The drug that her personal physician Sir Richard Reynolds prescribed was a tincture of cannabis and alcohol, and came with careful instructions. Still, Reynolds sang the praises of the drug in the inaugural issue of the now-celebrated medical journal *The Lancet*, writing that cannabis, "when pure and administered carefully, is one of the most valuable medicines we possess."

One doctor in particular became an early champion of cannabis. W.B. O'Shaughnessy was first introduced to the drug, like most of us, when he went away to college. While working as an assistant professor at the Medical College of Calcutta he heard stories of this wondrous folk remedy, and began conducting experiments on dogs and other animals. He concluded from these tests that the drug would be harmless to humans, and started testing it on some patients. In 1839, he wrote the first modern medical paper on the value of cannabis, concluding that it was an excellent analgesic and "an anticonvulsive remedy of the greatest value."

O'Shaughnessy's work turned the medical community onto cannabis and soon the drug was commonly prescribed by doctors throughout Europe and North America. In the meantime, France had grown as a center for cannabis culture, all because of Napoléon's foray into Turkish-ruled Egypt. He led his troops there in 1798, in hopes of smashing Britain's trade links to the Middle East. While Egypt fell to him, Napoléon lost his fleet in the process, and he and his army were stranded in the country. During their stay, Napoléon's troops were introduced to one of the local treats, hashish, and despite the Little Emperor's strict prohibition of its use, many soldiers soon fell in love with the drug.

The soldiers brought their newly acquired taste for cannabis home with them and introduced it to France, a scenario which would be repeated 170 years later, as Vietnam vets returned to the U.S.A. with shattered spirits and a newly honed taste for drugs. At first, hashish use was limited to a small circle of French veterans and their friends, but in time it spilled into popular culture. Again, the similarities to the U.S. in the 1960s are remarkable. Intellectuals and artists were the first to experiment with cannabis, and their interest soon trickled down to influence a generation of students.

The Hash-Eaters Club

Dr. Jacques-Joseph Moreau, a noted psychologist, spearheaded the movement. In the 1840s, Moreau began experimental cannabis treatments on mental patients, and was first impressed with the drug's positive effects; it seemed to calm the patients and relieve related problems such as headaches, appetite loss, anxiety, and sleep disorders. So in 1845 he formed the *Club de Hashishins*—"The Hash-Eaters Club"—with his friend Théophile Gautier, a writer and leading cultural figure, best known for coining the battle cry of the bohemian, "art for art's sake." The club was inspired by the romantic Orientalism fashionable at the time, and was dedicated to looking into the

THE HISTORY OF DRUGS

A Long, Remarkable Voyage

Charles Baudelaire (1821–1867) was a French poet, translator, and literary critic. The following excerpt is from "The Poem of Hashish," published in 1860. Although Baudelaire downplays the detrimental aspects of the drug, he eventually denounced hashish for its disturbing side effects.

Here is the drug we have before us: a morsel of green paste, the size of a nut, the smell of which is so potent that it gives rise to a certain repulsion and bouts of nausea, as will, for that matter, any fine and even appealing scent when carried to its maximum concentration and density, as it were. I might mention in passing that this proposition can be reversed, so that the vilest, most repugnant odor might perhaps become pleasurable were it reduced to its minimum of quantity and expansion. Here, then, is happiness!—it can be contained within an ordinary teaspoon!—happiness with all of its rapture, childishness, and folly! Swallow it without fear; you will not die of it. Your inner organs will suffer no harm. Later, perhaps, a too frequent invocation of the spell will diminish your power of resolve, perhaps you will be less a man than you are today, but the punishment is yet so distant and the future disaster of a nature so difficult to define! Where is the risk? Tomorrow, a slight touch of nervous exhaustion perhaps. Do you not each day risk greater chastisements for less recompense? So the matter is settled: To allow the drug its full range of expansion, you have dissolved your quantity of rich extract in a cup of strong coffee. You have arranged to take it on an empty stomach, postponing your dinner until at least nine or ten o'clock, to allow the poison free reign of action. In an hour a light soup alone will be tolerable. You are now sufficiently bolstered for a long, remarkable voyage. The steam whistle blows, the sails are set, and you, among all the other travelers, are a privileged exception, for you alone are unaware of your destination. You wished it to be so; long live destiny!

Charles Baudelaire, *Artificial Paradises*, trans. Stacy Diamond. New York: Carol, 1996.

non-medicinal value of cannabis. Thanks in part to Gautier's literary connections, the *Club de Hashishins* soon became the toast of Paris. Members would arrive dressed in their finest Oriental silks, and were offered a spoonful of a greenish jelly infused with hashish. Such literary luminaries as Arthur Rimbaud, Paul Verlaine, and Charles Baudelaire were regulars at the club's once-a-month meetings, and wrote glowing reports about their drug experiences. Baudelaire, in his essay "On Wine and Hashish," wrote of the highs and lows of a hashish trip, with "all joy and happiness being super abundant, all sorrow and anguish immensely profound." He also cautioned against using it when you have pressing matters at hand, or are feeling down in the dumps: "Any problem or worry, any memory of work claiming your will or attention at a particular time, will sound a knell across your intoxication and poison your pleasure."

It began with the best of intentions, but the *Club de Hashishins* did more damage than good to cannabis' otherwise sterling reputation. Gautier and Baudelaire would both eventually denounce the drug, finding its effects too disturbing. "Wine makes men happy and sociable; hashish isolates them," Baudelaire wrote. "Wine exalts the will; hashish annihilates it." Of course, these literary dogs were eating pure hash, and if they were expecting a mild beer buzz, they were certainly barking up the wrong tree. The result was that the public came to understand the cannabis drug only in its most potent form— imagine if we only knew alcohol from the stories of people who drank 100-proof rum—and a kind of hash hysteria was born. Following his death, rumors persisted that Baudelaire had succumbed to a hashish overdose. It was syphilis that really did him in, but the damage was done. Cannabis was now the thrill *dejour*, the *de rigueur* danger of France's dilettante set.

Experimental Use

Despite the bad press, the experimental use of cannabis extended to other Western countries, including the U.S. where

Fitz Hugh Ludlow's firsthand account *The Hasheesh Eater* titillated readers, and Britain, where members of London's Rhymers Club used hashish in order to create a sense of the occult. While the Rhymers Club lacked the punch of its French counterpart—the poet and playwright W.B. Yeats was the only famous member—it did help create an image of cannabis as a drug that could be dangerous if it found its way into the wrong hands. Yeats makes some brief mentions of his "haschisch" experiences in his autobiography *The Trembling of the Veil.* He and his lover Maud Gonne are known to have experimented with hashish, hoping to improve their telepathic powers. Another Rhymer, Arthur Symons, wrote the biography about fellow Rhymer Ernest Dowson and described one afternoon when Dowson served "tea, cakes, cigarettes and then hashish."

While the Rhymers were experimenting with pot, the medical community was also busy with some testing of its own. British doctors subjected cannabis to rigorous scientific scrutiny, and more than one hundred papers were published in learned journals exploring and espousing the drug's benefits. In the U.S., cannabis was listed in the *Pharmacopoeia,* the bible of medical drug use, and free samples were even offered to visitors at the 1876 American Centennial Exhibition in Washington. Remarkably though, the drug swiftly fell from grace. Within a few years into the new century, doctors were no longer prescribing the drug, and shortly after that, governments were declaring it a dangerous drug that was unraveling the moral rolling paper of society. The old high had reached a new low. What happened?

Falling Out of Favor

They say that the grass is always greener on the other side of the fence, and that old adage is never truer than when it's applied to medical science. Doctors are always looking for more effective treatments, and today's wonder drug can quickly become yesterday's news. Such was the case of cannabis. Physicians stopped prescribing it, not because of some great government conspiracy, but simply out of an earnest desire to improve the quality of care for their patients.

The scientific world had always had a problem with cannabis because its effects were rather unpredictable. In part, this was because the drug is difficult to process, so the potency varied from one dose to the next. As well, each patient seemed to react differently to the drug. To a scientific community, these inconstancies were disturbing indeed. Another problem with cannabis derivatives was that, unlike opiates, they weren't water soluble, so they couldn't be used in a hypodermic needle, which was invented in the 1850s. The final straw was the arrival of synthetic drugs such as aspirin, various barbiturates, and chloral hydrate, which, although arguably more harmful than cannabis, were much more chemically stable and therefore had more predictable effects on patients. All told, these developments pushed pot to the very bottom of the medical bag of tricks.

At the same time, cannabis was facing attacks on other fronts. Certainly, its reputation as a recreational drug was tainted thanks to its rejection from the members of the hashish clubs, and through the distortions the British government presented to support its Indian Hemp Tax. But the humble hemp industry was fading in the face of advancing technologies. It started with the advent of the cotton gin in 1800, which allowed for a cheaper fiber source. Over the next hundred years, sailboats gave way to steamships, and hemp was pushed further aside.[1] Soon, the use of hemp would plummet, and as the world looked to new sources of fiber, for the first time in history people wondered if *Cannabis sativa* had anything useful to offer.

---

1. Hemp woven into rope had previously been heavily used for ships.

A Review of the 1894 Indian Hemp Drugs Commission Report

Oriana Josseau Kalant

By the mid–nineteenth century, India was the British Empire's most lucrative colony, largely because of the tax the British had imposed in 1798 on all hemp products there. Marijuana played a large role in the social and religious lives of Indians, and the British knew that taxing the trade of bhang (leaves), ganja (buds), and charas (hashish) would bring in large revenues. By the 1870s, however, local administrators in India began to put pressure on the British Parliament to consider the ethical implications of marijuana use in India. Rumors that marijuana use led to insanity abounded, and many began to wonder whether the drug threatened India's moral fabric. Parliament finally conceded to the pressure in 1893, appointing a special commission, made up of both British and Indian administrators and medical experts, to analyze the cultivation, consumption, and effects of marijuana use throughout India. After nearly two years of rigorous research, the Indian Hemp Drugs Commission published a massive seven-volume report in 1894. This report remains the most extensive analysis of marijuana use ever conducted in a particular area, and it is remarkably relevant to questions about marijuana use even today. In the following excerpt, published in 1972, Oriana Josseau Kalant summarizes the commission's findings. The commission reported that little or no physical harm was caused by moderate marijuana use. It

Oriana Josseau Kalant, "Report of the Indian Hemp Drugs Commission, 1893–94: A Critical Review," *International Journal of the Addictions*, vol. 7, 1972, pp. 82–83, 85–91. Copyright © 1972 by Marcel Dekker, Inc. Reproduced by permission.

also found that claims that using the drug caused mental illness or criminal behavior were highly exaggerated. The commission's final opinion was that a prohibition of bhang, ganja, and charas in India was not justifiable. Kalant (1920–2001) was an internationally respected scientist who researched and wrote extensively about drugs and addiction. She authored *Drugs, Society, and Personal Choice* in 1972 and edited an anthology called *Cannabis: Health Risks* in 1983.

Having to assess the effects of cannabis from the testimony of a heterogeneous group of witnesses, the Commission adopted a commendably critical attitude. They submitted the evidence to close scrutiny, taking into account the qualifications and specific knowledge and objectivity of each witness. As they put it: "It has been deemed necessary, therefore, to make an effort to sift and test the evidence." Most witnesses had strongly biased opinions, but lacked real knowledge or familiarity with the use of the drugs:

> Some witnesses know only the medicinal use of the drugs, and are prepared to say nothing but good of them, being really ignorant of their use as intoxicants. . . . There are also witnesses who do know the use of the drugs as intoxicants, but know only the moderate use. They have nothing stronger to say of the drugs than would be said of alcohol by the man who only had seen a glass of wine taken at his own table or at the table of a friend. He knows nothing of the effects of excess. Others again have only experience of excessive consumption. . . . They feel towards these drugs as that man feels towards alcohol whose experience has been mainly gained among the social wrecks of the lowest parts of a great city.

This section contains a review of the physiological and psychological actions as they were then understood, and descriptions of the clinical effects, which do not differ appreciably from other accounts written in the 19th and 20th centuries. . . .

Only the evidence given by European and native [Indian] medical men was considered. It indicates clearly that many physicians knew little or nothing about the use of cannabis and even less about its possible physical harmful effects. This is made quite clear by the contrast between the written evidence and the oral cross examination. The evidence, particularly on the harmful effects of moderate use, was found [in the commission's report] ". . . to be in the highest degree defective". Half the witnesses considered that bronchitis, asthma, and dysentery were associated with moderate use of cannabis, and half believed they were not. Cross examination of the witnesses who believed in such an association skewed that their opinions were based on hearsay, on failure to distinguish between moderate and excessive use, or between coexistence and a cause-effect relationship of the habit and the illness, and on lack of awareness that the drugs were used to treat asthma and bronchitis. The Commission concluded that little or no harm resulted from moderate use of bhang [leaves], ganja [buds], or charas [hashish]. About excessive use of ganja and charas they say [in the Commission's report]: "As with long-continued and excessive cigarette smoking considerable bronchial irritation and chronic catarrhal laryngitis may be induced, so too, may a similar condition be caused by excessive ganja and charas smoking."

The evidence did not support the alleged connection between the use of cannabis and dysentery. But excessive use might indirectly cause gastrointestinal and other infections because of malnutrition due to loss of appetite or to diversion of income from food to the drugs.

Exaggerated Reports on the Mental Effects of Marijuana

Of all the alleged effects of cannabis, the most widely believed was that it could or often did produce psychotic illness, particularly if used excessively. Some witnesses even considered this the inevitable result of such use. Therefore particular importance was attached to this aspect of the inquiry. Considering the inherent difficulties in establishing the cause of mental illness generally, the Commission felt that this belief was possibly based on the following factors. It is easier to attribute causality to physical factors than to mental factors and predisposing mental states, because the former are concrete and may be more immediately associated with the onset of the illness. Among physical factors it is easiest to assign a causal role to a drug which, like cannabis, produces acute effects that closely resemble psychotic symptoms. The Commission felt that this popular belief had been greatly strengthened and made authoritative by the attitudes of the superintendents of mental hospitals in India who [according to the Commission's report]

> . . . have known nothing of the effects of the drugs at all, though the consumption is so extensive, except that cases of insanity have been brought to them attributed with apparent authority to hemp drugs. They have generalized from this limited and one-sided experience. They have concluded that hemp drugs produce insanity in every case, or in the great majority of cases, of consumption. They have had no idea that in the vast majority of cases this result does not follow the use. They have accordingly without sufficient inquiry assisted by the statistics they have supplied and by the opinions they have expressed in stereotyping the popular opinion and giving it authority and permanence.

Because the cross examination revealed the utterly inadequate knowledge of the medical witnesses, the Commission based its investigation exclusively on the records of the mental hospitals. Preliminary examination revealed that the procedure used to compile hospital records was also highly unreliable. Besides bureaucratic errors, the major difficulty was that the patients' histories, including statements about the cause of the condition, were not taken in the hospitals, but as a general rule by a police magistrate prior to certification. In the Commission's words: "The information consists often merely of the guesses of police officers as to the history and habits of a friendless and homeless wanderer". Therefore the Commission demanded a re-examination of the records of all the cases of psychosis attributed to cannabis for 1892, and based its final evaluation on the revised statistics.

These listed 222 of 1344 admissions as cannabis psychoses. The Commission concluded that in only 98 cases, or 7.3% of all admissions, was the association between cannabis use and the illness reasonably well documented. In 37 of these, other contributory factors (e.g., heredity, use of other drugs) were considered likely to have played a role, leaving 61 cases (or 4.5% of all admissions) of a presumably simple association between cannabis use and the psychoses. This association, however, did not necessarily mean that cannabis was the cause of the illness because use preceding the psychosis was not clearly established and because intemperance may be an early manifestation of mental illness rather than its cause. However, the Commission felt ". . . justified in accepting these 98 cases of the year 1892 as reasonably attributable, in whole or in part, to the use of hemp drugs" [according to their report].

The differential diagnosis of cannabis psychosis was also hampered by lack of precise information. Manic states were the most common syndromes, but with the possible exception of their shorter duration, they were indistinguishable from endogenous manic states, and therefore the differential diagnosis depended entirely on the history. The Commission was characteristically cautious in its conclusion:

> . . . we have a number of instances where the hemp drug habit has been so established in relation to the insanity that, admitting (as we must admit) that hemp drugs as intoxicants cause more or less of cerebral stimulation, it may be accepted as reasonably proved, in the absence of evidence of other cause, that hemp drugs do cause insanity.

Cannabis and Criminal Behavior

Two issues were considered: the social behavior of users, and the connection between cannabis use and crime.

Most witnesses thought that the behavior of moderate users was inconspicuous and generally inoffensive, and that even heavy users were rarely unpleasant or dangerous compared to heavy alcohol users. Some objections raised were that heavy users constituted a bad example for the young, and that the smell of ganja smoke and the frequent coughing and spitting by users were unpleasant.

In relation to crime, the Commission distinguished between incidence of criminal behavior in habitual users and unpremeditated crimes of violence committed during the acute intoxication. The proportion of psychopaths among moderate or even heavy users was not large and there was no specific connection between cannabis use and criminal behavior. The explanation for the minority view that such a connection did exist, was that use as such was considered antisocial behavior by some, and that criminal behavior and cannabis use were coincidental with low social status. Generally it was considered that cannabis use *per se* was not necessarily connected with crime. The allegation that cannabis was used in preparation for premeditated crimes, or to stupefy potential victims, was not confirmed. The Commission concluded: "There seems, therefore, good reason for believing that the connection between hemp drugs and ordinary crime is very slight indeed".

Most witnesses had no personal knowledge of heavy use of cannabis causing unpremeditated crimes of violence, although they were familiar with the connection between these crimes and the use of alcohol. In fact some felt that cannabis use had the opposite effect. The Commission itself judged that:

> It is probably safe to say in view of all the evidence that the tendency of the drugs often seems to be to develop or bring into play the natural disposition of the consumer, to emphasize his characteristics, or to assist him in obtaining what he sets his mind on. If he aims at ease and rest and he is let alone, he will be quiet and restful; but if he is naturally excitable and ill tempered, or if he is disturbed and crossed, he may be violent.

This issue was sufficiently important to warrant examination of the minority evidence in greater detail. The witnesses were asked to document their direct personal knowledge of homicides caused by cannabis use. From all of India and covering a period of many years, 81 cases were obtained. Fifty-eight cases, whose records were not directly examined by the Commission, included 17 instances of soldiers or armed police, ". . . to whom great temptation to violence presents itself when they are suddenly or seriously provoked", and 10 fakirs. The remaining 31 included cases where there was enough motive for the crime regardless of the use of cannabis, or where the drug was considered the cause of the crime simply because the criminal was known to be a user. From the group of 23 whose records were investigated, 19 were eliminated because of inadequate evidence, leaving only 4 instances of a reasonably clear causal connection between cannabis intoxication and the commission of the crime. These witnesses had based their claims on hearsay, vague impressions, and preconceptions. The Commission remarked:

> It is instructive to see how preconceived notions based on rumor and tradition tend to preserve the impression of certain particulars, while the impressions of far more important features of the case are completely forgotten.

The Commission's Conclusions

The Commission concluded that occasional use of moderate doses of cannabis for medicinal purposes, or habitual moderate use, produce no appreciable physical harmful effects except in unusual cases, and may even be beneficial. Heavy use of cannabis, as of other drugs, tends to make the user more susceptible to diseases such as bronchitis, associated with the inhalation of smoke, and dysentery through indirect causes.

Moderate cannabis use does not produce mental illness except in predisposed individuals. Excessive use, on the other hand, indicates and intensifies mental instability, and thus may contribute to the development of psychotic illness. Although this risk has been greatly exaggerated, [the Commission's report states] ". . . that [the drugs] do sometimes produce insanity seems beyond question."

Moderate cannabis use is not accompanied by any "moral injury" but heavy use "both indicates and intensifies moral weakness or depravity." From a social point of view even the heavy user is ordinarily inoffensive, although the habit may lead him to extreme poverty and dishonest practices, and in exceptionally rare cases to violent crimes.

Moderate use was the rule, and the harmful effects of heavy use were confined almost exclusively to the user. The socially harmful effects of excessive use were evidently insignificant, because most witnesses were unable to produce concrete evidence about them. . . .

The Commission concluded that the prohibition of bhang was "totally unjustifiable" because its use was ancient and deeply entrenched in social and religious customs; that moderate use was harmless and that excessive use was not as harmful as the excessive use of alcohol; that prohibition would be extremely difficult to enforce because of the wild growth of the plant, and that even if it were enforceable it would lead to the use "of more harmful stimulants;" and that it would be a very unpopular measure leading to widespread discontent— "The utmost that is necessary in regard to this product is that it should be brought under more effective control" [says the Commission's report].

Prohibition of ganja and charas was also considered unjustifiable. Although the effects of excessive use were assessed as harmful, neither their nature nor their extent were sufficient to justify prohibition. Enforcing the prohibition of imported charas would have been relatively easy, but not that of the locally produced ganja. The opinions of the witnesses were also taken into account. Although not specifically asked to give an opinion on this point, 574 volunteered one: 99 were in favor of prohibition and 475 against. The main reasons in favor were that the drugs were harmful; that all intoxicants, including cannabis, should be prohibited; and that such a measure would not give rise to significant social unrest. On the other hand, the majority against prohibition felt that it was impossible and unnecessary, that it would produce strong resentment among religious mendicants, that it was a politically dangerous measure, and that it would lead to the use of datura and other drugs. It was also considered [in the Commission's report] that to suppress the use of cannabis and not that of alcohol ". . . would be misunderstood by a large number of persons who believe, and apparently not without reason, that more harm is done in this country by the latter than by the former".

Having discarded prohibition as unjustifiable and unfeasible, the Commission set the aims of government intervention at discouraging excessive use as much as possible in order to protect the public health. Whatever measures the government took, they should ensure that the legitimate use of the drugs by the poor was not interfered with and that the illicit use of cannabis or of more harmful drugs was not encouraged.

These aims could best be achieved by a fair and consistent system of taxation of cannabis drugs designed to ". . . control their use, and especially their harmful use, in such a manner as to avoid a worse evil, and, subject to this proviso, to tax them as fully as possible" [suggests the report].

To achieve these aims the Commission made a thorough examination of the prevailing systems of administration of cannabis drugs across the country and a series of detailed recommendations based on the following principles. Taxation should be adequate. Cultivation should be centralized and permitted only under license. The extent of legal possession and the number of retail outlets should be limited, and the method adopted should be as uniform as possible throughout British India.

CHAPTER TWO

America's Introduction to Marijuana

Racism Fuels Fears About Marijuana

Ernest L. Abel

In the following excerpt from *Marihuana: The First Twelve Thousand Years*, Ernest L. Abel argues that antimarijuana sentiment and legislation in America during the 1920s and 1930s were incited by the racist assumptions of journalists and lawmakers. Both tended to characterize Mexican immigrants as degenerate, often violent, users of marijuana. In reality, Mexicans had become scapegoats for the economic problems of the Great Depression. Willing to work for low wages from large growers, Mexicans inadvertently contributed to the collapse of small farms in the Southwest. In addition, local governments complained about the number of unemployed Mexicans on relief. The depictions of Mexicans as marijuana addicts increased, and these immigrants were accused of spreading vice throughout the country. In the 1930s the American government responded by repatriating many Mexicans. Not surprisingly, this new culture of drug paranoia spread from the border towns to the big cities such as New Orleans and New York, where marijuana became negatively associated with jazz music and African Americans. However false the hyperbolic reports, many Americans began to fear marijuana's purported dangers. Ernest L. Abel is a Canadian doctor, professor, and author of many books on drugs and diseases, including *Alcohol Wordlore and Folklore, Psychoactive Drugs and Sex,* and *A Marihuana Dictionary.*

Even when it was not against the law, marihuana was used by very few Americans. Those who used it were typically from minority groups like the Mexicans and the Negros, and this made them and their drug preferences highly visible. The fact that these people smoked marihuana for pleasure made marihuana a vice that was doubly suspect, since the American work ethic never recognized anything like an "artificial paradise."

At the root of America's preoccupation with the potential dangers of drugs such as marihuana was a xenophobia that seems to characterize the history of the country almost from its very beginnings. Although settled by foreigners, native-born Americans blamed newcomers to the United States for many of the country's ills. In the late nineteenth and early twentieth century, newly arrived foreigners were blamed for the sprawling urban slums, depressed paychecks, and labor unrest—conditions beyond the ken of frontier America's whelps. Although America was built by the sweat of toiling immigrants, the newcomers were seldom welcomed. This was especially true when the blue-eyed, blond-haired, fair-skinned, Protestant migrations gave way to the brown- and green-eyed, black-haired, swarthy, non-Protestants from Southern and Eastern Europe who settled in the coastal cities of America.

Penniless when they arrived, they were grateful for whatever jobs they could get. Their readiness to toil for the lowest of wages was seen by native Americans as a stab in the back. These foreigners, they felt, were nothing less than strikebreakers.

In the southwest, the sudden increase in Mexican immigration to the United States around 1910 set off yet another round of ethnic confrontation. The Mexicans were lower-class immigrants. They were crude, loud, uneducated. They lived in dirty shanties, ate strange food, and spoke a foreign language. The more resentful of these foreigners Americans became, the readier they were to attribute other negative characteristics to the Mexican. The fact that the Mexicans were Catholics made their situation even more touchy since Protestant America considered Catholicism a religion of dark superstition and ignorance.

The Mexican was the Negro of the southwestern United States. While not a slave or a sharecropper, he was a peasant. The stereotype of the Mexican was that of a thief, an untamed savage, hot-blooded, quick to anger yet inherently lazy and irresponsible. . . .

When the 1930s devastated the American economy, the Mexicans bore the brunt of the scapegoat mentality in the southwest. Everything about them was abhorrent to many Americans, and there was a general hew and cry to kick them out of the country. Harassment was commonplace. The Mexicans were censured for almost everything they did or failed to do, including smoking marihuana. Marihuana, in fact, became the pretext for vexing the Mexicans just as opium had been the pretext for vexing the Chinese years before. . . .

A History of Resentment

In 1910, the revolution south of the Rio Grande drove thousands of Mexicans north into the United States. The main border crossings were El Paso, Texas; Nogales and Douglas, Arizona; and Calexico, California. The immigrants who passed through these points of entry usually took up temporary residence on the outskirts of these towns, and the Mexican ghetto or barrio became a common sight in parts of the southwest.

At first the newcomers were welcomed, especially by the wealthy landowners and the railway companies. These people were willing to work for cheap wages. As bad as the pay was, it was still worse in Mexico. While many Mexicans were ferried as far north as Chicago to work in the rail yards, most were recruited as fruit and vegetable pickers in California's Imperial and San Joaquin Valleys, in Texas's Rio Grande Valley, in Arizona's Salt River Valley, and in the sugar beet fields of Colorado. So valuable a labor commodity were the Mexicans that big business pressured Congress to exclude them from the literacy test and head-tax payments that had been written into the Immigration Act of 1917.

Small businessmen also reaped dollars from the newcomers, and as late as 1930 they fought all attempts to restrict Mexican immigration. . . .

Small farmers, unable to compete with large growers because of the cheap wages paid to the Mexicans, were being driven out of business. Labor unions likewise complained of the competition from cheap labor. Local governments were unhappy about the numbers of Mexcians on relief. Business interests countered that the Mexicans were the most preferable of all the cheap labor available and were more suited than American whites at working at menial tasks. Caught in the middle, the Mexicans became the scapegoats for the economic conflict between business and labor. It was largely in this role of monkey-in-the-middle that the habits and customs of the Mexicans began to be attacked as un-American, and at the top of the list of un-American-like activities was their use of marihuana.

As the numbers of Mexican immigrants began to increase, especially in the border towns of the southwest, they were the object of close scrutiny by the townsfolk. Suspicious and often resentful of these newcomers, the townspeople humiliated, harassed, and abused them to make them feel as unwelcome as possible. When the Mexicans lashed back at their tormentors, their actions were often attributed to the influence of marihuana, which to many Americans symbolized the Mexican presence in America.

Early Ordinances Against Marihuana

As early as 1914, the town of El Paso [Texas] passed a local ordinance outlawing the sale or possession of marihuana. Like the outlawing of opium, the ordinance was meant to annoy and harass a class of people. The pretext for the law was said to have been a fight started by a Mexican who was allegedly under the influence of the drug, but the real reason was dislike, if not hatred, of the foreigners from across the Rio Grande.

Relations between Americans and Mexicans were not helped

very much by the antics of the Mexican revolutionary Pancho Villa. Villa frequently led his bandits on raids against towns on the American side of the Rio Grande and then fled back into Mexico. When finally the Americans had had enough, they sent General "Black Jack" Pershing in pursuit of the elusive bandit.

When Pershing returned from Mexico, there was some concern that marihuana had infiltrated the American ranks, although an official inquiry failed to turn up any proof to that effect. However, in 1921, the commandant of Fort Sam Houston expressly forbade marihuana anywhere on the grounds of the military post, ostensibly because American soldiers were smoking the drug while on duty.

In 1916, military authorities in the Panama Canal Zone began to suspect that army personnel were also smoking marihuana, but little attention was given to the issue at that time.

Six years later, in 1922, the provost marshall became concerned about reports that American soldiers were smoking marihuana and were becoming disobedient as a result. The following year, the army prohibited possession of marihuana by American personnel in the Canal Zone. . . .

Mexicans, Marihuana, and Violence

As the most conspicuous users of marihuana, Mexicans were often-times accused of being incited to violence by the drug. A letter written in 1911 by the American consul at Nogales, Mexico, stated that marihuana "causes the smoker to become exceedingly pugnacious and to run amuck without discrimination." A Texas police captain claimed that under marihuana's baneful influence, Mexicans become "very violent, especially when they become angry and will attack an officer even if a gun is drawn on him. They seem to have no fear, I have also noted that when under the influence of this weed they have enormous strength and that it will take several men to handle one man while under ordinary circumstances one man could handle him with ease.". . .

When challenged, these statements were never supported. Dr. M.V. Ball, one of America's few authorities on marihuana, visited the border towns in 1922 as a representative of the American Medical Association to get a firsthand look at the alleged dangers of marihuana to the citizenry. Ball had previously noted that whenever cannabis drugs were mentioned in the old scientific literature, they were invariably mixed with opium, and he was skeptical of the reports he had heard about the drug as far as its criminogenic properties were concerned.

During a site visit to a Texas jail, the warden gave an inmate a marihuana cigarette to smoke so that Ball could see for himself what it did to a man. "To the surprise of the American Prison Physician and the jailer who assured me three wiffs would drive fellows so wild that they become exceptionally difficult to subdue," the smoker remained calm and unperturbed. "There is no evidence whatever that I can discover," Ball subsequently reported, "to warrant the belief that marihuana smoking is on the increase among Americans or that it is prevalent or common, there is no evidence worthy of belief that marihuana is a habit forming weed or drug, or that its use is increasing among Mexicans in Mexico or in America."

Four years later, Dr. W.W. Stockberger, a scientist at the U.S. Bureau of Plant Industry, issued a similar statement. "We have had correspondence with El Paso and other border cities in Texas for a good many years about this situation," he said. However, "the reported effects of the drug on Mexicans, making them want to clean up the town [commit crimes], do not jibe very well with the effects of cannabis, which so far as we have reports, simply causes temporary elation, followed by depression and heavy sleep. . . ."

During the 1930s the most sensationalistic of all the crimes to be attributed to marihuana's baneful influence was that of the death of a Florida family. On October 16, 1933, Victor Licata axed his mother, father, two brothers, and a sister to death in their Tampa home. The following day the Tampa chief of police declared "war on the marihuana traffic here," after reading the investigating officer's report that "the weed used as a cigarette had been indirectly to blame for the wholesale murder of the Michael Licata family. . . ." The link between the crime and marihuana was that Victor Licata had been a known user of marihuana. . . .

Licata was ultimately sentenced to the Florida state mental hospital, where he was . . . examined and diagnosed as suffering from a long-lasting psychosis which was probably responsible for his crime. In 1950, Licata hanged himself.

Prejudice Affects Law Enforcement

Although there was no evidence to show that Licata had killed his family while under the influence of marihuana, Harry Anslinger, the commissioner of the Bureau of Narcotics, cited the case during the hearings on the Marihuana Tax Act of 1937 as just one example of the dangers of marihuana. . . .

In his book *The Murderers*, Anslinger once again turned to the Licata case:

> Much of the most irrational juvenile violence and killing that has written a new chapter of shame and tragedy is traceable directly to this hemp intoxication. . . . A sixteen-year-old [sic] kills his entire family of five in Florida. . . . Every one of these crimes has been preceded by the smoking of one or more marihuana "reefers."

Anslinger's attitude was typical of other police officers in regard to the marihuana issue. Without any evidence to back them up, more than a few law enforcement officers adamantly denounced marihuana as a "killer drug."

The campaign against the drug picked up especially during the Depression as marihuana became yet another issue on which to harass Mexican immigrants. The Mexicans were accused of spreading the marihuana vice throughout the nation:

> While the plant is a native of the Torrid Zone, its cultivation has been taken up through the United States and it is, at the present time, to be found in practically every state in the

Union—in fact wherever Mexicans are located. So far north and east of its natural habitat has the weed spread under cultivation, that the New York Narcotics Forces have discovered patches of it which were grown within the city limits. Again the Mexican influence is shown, the supply being found near the Pennsylvania Railroad Yards, in the Borough of Queens, where the Mexicans are employed.

Labor groups and antiforeigner groups like the American Coalition badgered California's legislators to kick the Mexicans out of the state on grounds that marihuana was undermining American morality. Said C.M. Goethe, a spokesman for the coalition:

Marihuana, perhaps now the most insidious of our narcotics, is a direct by-product of unrestricted Mexican immigration. Easily grown, it has been asserted that it has recently been planted between rows in a California penitentiary garden. Mexican peddlers have been caught distributing sample marihuana cigarets to school children. Bills for our quota against Mexico have been blocked mysteriously in every Congress since the 1924 Quota Act. Our nation has more than enough laborers.

A report from the Missionary Educator Movement in California also called attention to the widespread usage of marihuana among the Mexicans and its alleged connection with lack of morality:

The use of marihuana is not uncommon in the colonies of the lower class of Mexican immigrants. This is a native drug made from what is sometimes called the "crazy weed." The effects are high exhiliration and intoxication, followed by extreme depression and broken nerves. [Police] officers and Mexicans both ascribe many of the moral irregularities of Mexicans to the effects of marihuana.

Los Angeles's chief of detectives, Joseph F. Taylor, likewise hammered away at the crime-inducing effects of marihuana on the Mexican:

In the past we have had officers of this department shot and killed by marihuana addicts and have traced the act of murder directly to the influence of marihuana, with no other motive.

Elsewhere throughout the southwest, where there were heavy concentrations of Mexicans, newspapers [such as a June 11, 1930, edition of the *Tulsa Tribune*] carried on a vigorous campaign against marihuana, aimed ostensibly at the evils of the drug but the real object of their indictment was crystal clear: "Four men, including a deputy sheriff, were seriously injured last night by a marihuana-raged Mexican before the bullets of another officer killed him, as he charged this officer with a knife."

In 1933, the arrest of a "dope ring" specializing in marihuana, in Longmont, Colorado, prompted the remark from one journalist that marihuana was "highly intoxicating and constitutes an ever recurring problem where there are Mexicans or Spanish-Americans of the lower classes."

Readers were likewise informed [by the *New York Times* in 1934] that while "appalling in its effects on the human mind and body as narcotics, the consumption of marihuana appears to be proceeding, virtually unchecked in Colorado and other Western states with a large Spanish-American population." And if this were not dire warning enough, [according to scholar J. Helmer] readers were also told that marihuana was "kin to loco weed . . . [and] when mixed with hay causes death to horses!"

The Depression and Repatriation

In 1931, the California State Narcotic Committee reported that marihuana usage was "widespread throughout Southern California among the Mexican population there," and cited statistics from the city of Los Angeles that marihuana was frequently listed as being involved in criminal arrests. On the other hand, although "widespread" among the Mexicans, no other city in the state could produce comparable statistics. In fact, surveys of crime and delinquency among the Mexicans clearly demonstrated that they exhibited [according to J. Helmer] "delinquent tendencies less than their proportion of the population would entitle them to show." When the records of one officer who had been adamant in his denunciation of the Mexican crime wave were examined, it was discovered that he had overestimated the proportion of Mexican arrests by 60 percent!

It was not their antisocial behavior nor their use of marihuana that made the Mexicans *persona non grata*. As long as the economy had been viable, differences between the Mexicans and the Anglos were rarely belligerent. When the Depression hit, however, jobs in the city disappeared. Anglo workers now began looking to farm labor as a means of livelihood. It was then that real competition for jobs became an issue.

Relief programs for the unemployed were a related issue. During the 1920s, the Mexican population in Los Angeles alone increased by 226 percent. By 1930, there were over 97,000 Mexicans in the city. When these immigrants lost their jobs and went on relief, the business sector, which had once regarded them as an exploitable asset, now began to view them as an intolerable burden.

To reduce the relief burden, labor groups led by the AFL [American Federation of Labor] began urging that the Mexicans be shipped back across the border. Repatriation became law in the 1930s, and beginning in 1931 thousands of Mexicans were shipped back across the Rio Grande. The cost to repatriate one Mexican to Mexico City was $14.70. An average family ran about $71.14, including food and transportation. Los Angeles County paid out $77,249.29 to repatriate one covey of 6024 Mexicans and figured it had got itself a bargain compared to the $424,933.70 it estimated charitable relief would have cost had these people remained.

Mexicans who did not wish to return voluntarily were subjected to varying forms and degrees of harassment. Many were charged with vagrancy. Others were arrested for violation of state marihuana laws. When they began to resist efforts to jail and deport them, their resistance was attributed to the influence of marihuana and these charges lent further weight to the accusation that marihuana incited violence.

Marijuana: Assassin of Youth

Harry J. Anslinger

Harry J. Anslinger is often cited as the sole force behind the outlawing of marijuana in the United States. His government career began in the War and Treasury departments, but he made his real mark in 1930 as the first head of the Federal Bureau of Narcotics. Anslinger's years as a supporter of the failed prohibition of alcohol caused him to take an even harsher stance against other narcotics. He began his antimarijuana campaign at the state level, using sensationalistic and falsified newspaper stories to incite a general fear about the drug's eminence and effects. Anslingler published "Marijuana: Assassin of Youth" in *American Magazine* in 1937. Its dramatic evidence, however exaggerated, had a great impact on American readers and helped to generate support for antimarijuana legislation. In this excerpt from his article, Anslinger claims that marijuana causes violent, criminal behavior, particularly in youths. He also creates the impression that marijuana is an underestimated problem in nearly every city in America. Anslinger argues that the federal government should regulate the drug. Less than one year after the publication of this essay, Anslinger convinced Congress to pass the first piece of federal legislation specifically targeting marijuana: the Marihuana Tax Act of 1937, which required all those who dealt in marijuana to register and pay a heavy tax on it.

Harry J. Anslinger, "Marijuana: Assassin of Youth," *American Magazine*, vol. 124, 1937, pp. 18–19, 150–53.

The sprawled body of a young girl lay crushed on the sidewalk the other day after a plunge from the fifth story of a Chicago apartment house. Everyone called it suicide, but actually it was murder. The killer was a narcotic known to America as marijuana, and to history as hashish. It is a narcotic used in the form of cigarettes, comparatively new to the United States and as dangerous as a coiled rattlesnake.

How many murders, suicides, robberies, criminal assaults, holdups, burglaries, and deeds of maniacal insanity it causes each year, especially among the young, can be only conjectured. The sweeping march of its addiction has been so insidious that, in numerous communities, it thrives almost unmolested, largely because of official ignorance of its effects.

Here indeed is the unknown quantity among narcotics. No one can predict its effect. No one knows, when he places a marijuana cigarette to his lips, whether he will become a joyous reveler in a musical heaven, a mad insensate, a calm philosopher, or a murderer.

That youth has been selected by the peddlers of this poison as an especially fertile field makes it a problem of serious concern to every man and woman in America.

There was the young girl, for instance, who leaped to her death. Her story is typical. Some time before, this girl, like others of her age who attend our high schools, had heard the whispering of a secret which has gone the rounds of American youth. It promised a new thrill, the smoking of a type of cigarette which contained a "real kick." According to the whispers, this cigarette could accomplish wonderful reactions and with no harmful aftereffects. So the adventurous girl and a group of her friends gathered in an apartment, thrilled with the idea of doing "something different" in which there was "no harm." Then a friend produced a few cigarettes of the loosely rolled "homemade" type. They were passed from one to another of the young people, each taking a few puffs.

The results were weird. Some of the party went into paroxysms of laughter; every remark, no matter how silly, seemed excruciatingly funny. Others of mediocre musical ability became almost expert; the piano dinned constantly. Still others found themselves discussing weighty problems of youth with remarkable clarity. As one youngster expressed it, he "could see through stone walls." The girl danced without fatigue, and the night of unexplainable exhilaration seemed to stretch out as though it were a year long. Time, conscience, or consequences became too trivial for consideration.

Other parties followed, in which inhibitions vanished, conventional barriers departed, all at the command of this strange cigarette with its ropy, resinous odor. Finally there came a gathering at a time when the girl was behind in her studies and greatly worried. With every puff of the smoke the feeling of despondency lessened. Everything was going to be all right—at last. The girl was "floating" now, a term given to marijuana intoxication. Suddenly, in the midst of her laughter and dancing, she thought of her school problems. Instantly they were solved. Without hesitancy she walked to a window and leaped to her death. Thus can marijuana "solve" one's difficulties.

The cigarettes may have been sold by a hot tamale vendor or by a street peddler, or in a dance hall or over a lunch counter, or even from sources much nearer to the customer. The police of a Midwestern city recently accused a school janitor of having conspired with four other men, not only to peddle cigarettes to children, but even to furnish apartments where smoking parties might be held.

A Chicago mother, watching her daughter die as an indirect result of marijuana addiction, told officers that at least 50 of the girl's young friends were slaves to the narcotic. This means 50 unpredictables. They may cease its use; that is not so difficult as with some narcotics. They may continue addiction until they deteriorate mentally and become insane. Or they may turn to violent forms of crime, to suicide or to murder. Marijuana gives few warnings of what it intends to do to the human brain.

An Insidious History

The menace of marijuana addiction is comparatively new to America. In 1931, the marijuana file of the United States Narcotic Bureau was less than two inches thick, while today [in 1937] the reports crowd many large cabinets. Marijuana is a weed of the Indian hemp family, known in Asia as Cannabis Indica and in America as Cannabis Sativa. Almost everyone who has spent much time in rural communities has seen it, for it is cultivated in practically every state. Growing plants by the thousands were destroyed by law-enforcement officers last year [1936] in Texas, New York, New Jersey, Mississippi, Michigan, Maryland, Louisiana, Illinois, and the attack on the weed is only beginning. It was an unprovoked crime some years ago [1933] which brought the first realization that the age-old drug had gained a foothold in America. An entire family was murdered by a youthful addict in Florida.[1] When officers arrived at the home they found the youth staggering about in a human slaughterhouse. With an ax he had killed his father, his mother, two brothers, and a sister. He seemed to be in a daze.

"I've had a terrible dream," he said. "People tried to hack off my arms!"

"Who were they?" an officer asked.

"I don't know. Maybe one was my uncle. They slashed me with knives and I saw blood dripping from an ax."

He had no recollection of having committed the multiple crime. The officers knew him ordinarily as a sane, rather quiet young man; now he was pitifully crazed. They sought the reason. The boy said he had been in the habit of smoking something which youthful friends called "muggles:" a childish name for marijuana.

Since that tragedy there has been a race between the spread of marijuana and its suppression. Unhappily, so far, marijuana has won by many lengths. The years 1935 and

1. The murderer, Victor Licata, was ultimately sentenced to a Florida state mental hospital and diagnosed as suffering from a long-term psychosis.

1936 saw its most rapid growth in traffic. But at least we now know what we are facing. We know its history, its effects, and its potential victims. Perhaps with the spread of this knowledge the public may be aroused sufficiently to conquer the menace. Every parent owes it to his children to tell them of the terrible effects of marijuana to offset the enticing "private information" which these youths may have received. There must be constant enforcement and equally constant education against this enemy, which has a record of murder and terror running through the centuries.

The Spread of Marijuana

The weed was known to the ancient Greeks and it is mentioned in Homer's *Odyssey*. Homer wrote that it made men forget their homes and turned them into swine. Ancient Egyptians used it. In the year 1090, there was founded in Persia the religious and military order of the Assassins, whose history is one of cruelty, barbarity, and murder, and for good reason. The members were confirmed users of hashish, or marijuana, and it is from the Arabic "hashshashin" that we have the English word "assassin." Even the term "running amok" relates to the drug, for the expression has been used to describe natives of the Malay Peninsula who, under the influence of hashish, engage in violent and bloody deeds.

Marijuana was introduced into the United States from Mexico, and swept across America with incredible speed.

It began with the whispering of vendors in the Southwest that marijuana would perform miracles for those who smoked it, giving them a feeling of physical strength and mental power, stimulation of the imagination, the ability to be "the life of the party." The peddlers preached also of the weed's capabilities as a "love potion." Youth, always adventurous, began to look into these claims and found some of them true, not knowing that this was only half the story. They were not told that addicts may often develop a delirious rage during which they are temporarily and violently insane; that this insanity may take the form of a desire for self-destruction or a persecution complex to be satisfied only by the commission of some heinous crime.

Marijuana and Violent Behavior

It would be well for law-enforcement officers everywhere to search for marijuana behind cases of criminal and sex assault. During the last year [1937] a young male addict was hanged in Baltimore for criminal assault on a ten-year-old girl. His defense was that he was temporarily insane from smoking marijuana. In Alamosa, Colorado, a degenerate brutally attacked a young girl while under the influence of the drug. In Chicago, two marijuana-smoking boys murdered a policeman.

In at least two dozen other comparatively recent cases of murder or degenerate sex attacks, many of them committed by youths, marijuana proved to be a contributing cause. Perhaps you remember the young desperado in Michigan who, a few months ago, caused a reign of terror by his career of burglaries and holdups, finally to be sent to prison for life after kidnapping a Michigan state policeman, killing him, then handcuffing him to the post of a rural mailbox. This young bandit was a marijuana fiend.

A 16-year-old boy was arrested in California for burglary. Under the influence of marijuana he had stolen a revolver and was on the way to stage a holdup when apprehended. Then there was the 19-year-old addict in Columbus, Ohio, who, when police responded to a disturbance complaint, opened fire upon an officer, wounding him three times, and was himself killed by the returning fire of the police. In Ohio a gang of seven young men, all less than 20 years old, had been caught after a series of 38 holdups. An officer asked them where they got their incentive.

"We only work when we're high on tea," one explained.

"On what?"

"On tea. Oh, there are lots of names for it. Some people call it 'mu' or 'muggles' or 'Mary Weaver' or 'moocah' or 'weed' or 'reefers'—there's a million names for it."

"All of which mean marijuana?"

"Sure. Us kids got on to it in high school three or four years ago; there must have been 25 or 30 of us who started smoking it. The stuff was cheaper then; you could buy a whole tobacco tin of it for 50 cents. Now these peddlers will charge you all they can get, depending on how shaky you are. Usually though, it's two cigarettes for a quarter."

This boy's casual procurement of the drug was typical of conditions in many cities in America. He told of buying the cigarettes in dance halls, from the owners of small hamburger joints, from peddlers who appeared near high schools at dismissal time. Then there were the "booth joints" or Bar-B-Q stands, where one might obtain a cigarette and a sandwich for a quarter, and there were the shabby apartments of women who provided not only the cigarettes but rooms in which girls and boys might smoke them.

"But after you get the habit," the boy added, "you don't bother much about finding a place to smoke. I've seen as many as three or four high-school kids jam into a telephone booth and take a few drags."

The officer questioned him about the gang's crimes: "Remember that filling station attendant you robbed—how you threatened to beat his brains out?"

The youth thought hard. "I've got a sort of hazy recollection," he answered. "I'm not trying to say I wasn't there, you understand. The trouble is, with all my gang, we can't remember exactly what we've done or said. When you get to 'floating,' it's hard to keep track of things." "If I had killed somebody on one of those jobs, I'd never have known it," explained one youth. "Sometimes it was over before I realized that I'd even been out of my room."

Therein lies much of the cruelty of marijuana, especially in its attack upon youth. The young, immature brain is a thing of impulses, upon which the "unknown quantity" of the drug acts as an almost overpowering stimulant. There are numerous cases on record like that of an Atlanta boy who robbed his father's safe of thousands of dollars in jewelry and cash. Of high-school age, this boy apparently had been headed for an honest, successful career. Gradually, however, his father noticed a change in him. Spells of shakiness and nervousness would be succeeded by periods when the boy would assume a grandiose manner and engage in excessive, senseless laughter, extravagant conversation, and wildly impulsive actions. When these actions finally resulted in robbery the father went at his son's problem in earnest and found the cause of it—a marijuana peddler who catered to school children. The peddler was arrested.

It is this useless destruction of youth which is so heartbreaking to all of us who labor in the field of narcotic suppression. No one can predict what may happen after the smoking of the weed. . . .

Marijuana Blooms Everywhere

Reports from various sections of the country indicate that the control and sale of marijuana has not yet passed into the hands of the big gangster syndicates. The supply is so vast and grows in so many places that gangsters perhaps have found it difficult to dominate the sources. A big, hardy weed, with serrated, swordlike leaves topped by bunchy small blooms supported upon a thick, stringy stalk, marijuana has been discovered in almost every state. New York police uprooted hundreds of plants growing in a vacant lot in Brooklyn. In New York State alone last year 200 tons of the growing weed were destroyed. Acres of it have been found in various communities. Patches have been revealed in backyards, behind signboards, in gardens. In many places in the West it grows wild. Wandering dopesters gather the tops from along the right of way of railroads.

An evidence of how large the traffic may be came to light last year [1936] near LaFitte, Louisiana. Neighbors of an Italian family had become alarmed by wild stories told by the children of the family. They, it seemed, had suddenly become millionaires. They talked of owning inconceivable amounts of money, of automobiles they did not possess, of living in a palatial home. At last their absurd lies were reported to the police, who discovered that their parents were allowing them to smoke something that came from the tops of tall plants which their father grew on his farm. There was a raid, in which more than 500,000 marijuana plants were destroyed. This discovery led next day to another raid on a farm at Bourg, Louisiana. Here a crop of some 2,000 plants was found to be growing between rows of vegetables. The eight persons arrested confessed that their main source of income from this crop was in sales to boys and girls of high-school age.

With possibilities for such tremendous crops, grown secretly, gangdom has been hampered in its efforts to corner the profits of what has now become an enormous business. It is to be hoped that the menace of marijuana can be wiped out before it falls into the vicious protectorate of powerful members of the underworld.

A Federal Call to Arms

But to crush this traffic we must first squarely face the facts. Unfortunately, while every state except one has laws to cope with the traffic, the powerful right arm which could support these states has been all but impotent. I refer to the United States government. There has been no national law against the growing, the sale, or the possession of marijuana.

As this is written a bill to give the federal government control over marijuana has been introduced in Congress by Representative Robert L. Doughton of North Carolina, Chairman of the House Ways and Means Committee. It has the backing of Secretary of the Treasury Morgenthau, who has under his supervision the various agencies of the United States Treasury Department, including the Bureau of Narcotics, through which Uncle Sam fights the dope evil. It is a revenue bill, modeled after other narcotic laws which make use of the taxing power to bring about regulation and control.

The passage of such a law, however, should not be the signal for the public to lean back, fold its hands, and decide that all danger is over. America now faces a condition in which a new, although ancient, narcotic has come to live next door to us, a narcotic that does not have to be smuggled into the country. This means a job of unceasing watchfulness by every police department and by every public spirited civic organization. It calls for campaigns of education in every school, so that children will not be deceived by the wiles of peddlers, but will know of the insanity, the disgrace, the horror which marijuana can bring to its victim.

A Clinical Study of the Marijuana High

Samuel Allentuck and Karl M. Bowman

Samuel Allentuck and Karl M. Bowman were both established in their careers as practicing psychiatrists, researchers, and writers when they were asked to take part in Mayor Fiorello La Guardia's Committee on Marihuana, commissioned by the New York City mayor in response to overwhelmingly negative newspaper stories about rampant marijuana abuse in the city. The following paper, which they delivered at the annual meeting of the American Psychiatric Association in 1942, was based on the studies they conducted for the mayor. Their clinical description of the physical and mental effects of marijuana caused much discussion in both scientific and popular circles, for it undermined many of the accepted assumptions about cannabis intoxication. The physiological effects that their research subjects experienced were relatively mild. Although some users were prone to paranoia after ingestion, most characterized the psychological "high" of marijuana as a feeling of euphoria. Allentuck and Bowman report that marijuana is not as addictive as alcohol or tobacco, and they conclude that people use marijuana socially in much the same way as they use alcohol: to lower inhibitions and to accentuate personality traits already inherent in the user. They do not believe that marijuana is a stepping-stone to further drug use; in fact, the doctors advise further study of its potential medical applications.

Samuel Allentuck and Karl M. Bowman, "The Psychiatric Aspects of Marihuana Intoxication," *American Journal of Psychiatry*, vol. 99, September 1942, pp. 248–50.

Marihuana has been known as a passport to euphoria since ancient times. It has fascinated men of imagination, and descriptions of its effects upon the mind and body have been given in popular and scientific literature countless times. . . .

The active principle in the plant is an oil, occurring in maximum concentration in the flowering tops. The drug is ingested or inhaled after being prepared for use in various ways in different parts of the world. In this hemisphere it is usually smoked, but may be eaten in the form of a candy, or drunk in various liquid preparations. The strength and quality of the effect of marihuana vary with the geographical source of the plant. It is strongest in the African derivative, less strong in its Central American form, and weakest as found in the temperate zones of this country [the United States].

Physiological Effects

Marihuana is unique in the reactions it produces in its users, although its physiological effects have been likened to those of the atropine group of drugs, and its psychic effects to those of alcohol. The following is a clinical picture of the sequence of events resulting from the ingestion of marihuana. The sequence of events is the same whether the drug is ingested or inhaled, but the latter produces its effects more rapidly.

Within one-half to one hour after the ingestion of marihuana the conjunctiva reddens, the pupils dilate and react sluggishly to light. . . . Ophthalmoscopic examination reveals nothing unusual in the nerve head, vessels or retinal background. The vision for distance, proximity and color changes but slightly. The tongue becomes tremulous and dry, and the mouth and throat parched, suggesting a diminution in salivary secretion. Cardiovascular changes consist of an increase in the radial pulse rate and a rise in the blood pressure which closely follows the pulse increase. The extremities become tremulous, and there are involuntary twitching, hyperreflexia, increased sensitivity to touch, pressure and pain stimuli. . . . Not all of these phenomena occur in every subject, but when any of them does, it lasts for about twelve hours. Elaborate laboratory studies of the effects of marihuana intoxication for shorter and longer periods, on users and non-users, reveal no significant systemic alterations.

Psychological Effects

Mental phenomena arise two to three hours after ingestion, or almost immediately after inhalation of the drug. The subject admits being "high." This state is characterized by a sensation of "floating in air," "falling on waves," lightness or dizziness in the head, ringing in the ears, and heaviness in the limbs. Euphoria is first manifested objectively in volubility and increased psychomotor activity, and later subjectively in a delicious and confused lassitude. Distance and time intervals subjectively appear elastic. In three to six hours after ingestion of marihuana hunger, manifested mainly in a craving for sweets, and a feeling of fatigue and sleepiness become prominent. The individual may sleep from one to six hours and on awakening is "down"; that is, he no longer feels "high." The clinical phenomena may linger for another few hours.

The mental status usually reveals a hyperactive, apprehensive, loquacious, somewhat suspicious individual. His stream of talk may be circumstantial; his mood may be elevated, but he does not harbor frank abnormal mental content such as delusions, hallucinations, phobias or autistic thinking. Attention, concentration and comprehension are only slightly disturbed, as is evidenced by the fact that the results in his educational achievement tests are only slightly lowered. . . .

Limitations of time will not permit detailed description of the nine psychoses precipitated in our series of 77 subjects. However, it should be noted that a characteristic marihuana psychosis does not exist. Marihuana will not produce a psychosis *de novo* in a well-integrated, stable person. In unstable users the personality factor and the mood preceding the ingestion of marihuana will color any psychosis that may result. In no two of the cases developing psychoses in our series were the patterns similar. Marihuana psychosis is protean in its manifestations and may be mistaken for schizophrenic, affective, paranoic, organic, psychoneurotic or psychopathic reaction types. Should a psychosis be precipitated in an unstable personality it may last only a few hours or it may continue for a few weeks. It may be controlled by withdrawal of the drug and the administration of barbiturates. After a few hours of sleep following the psychotic episode treated with barbiturates, the patient may awaken with complete memory for his experience and with his insight unimpaired.

Prolonged Effects

The prolonged effects of the drug are strongly subjective, and consist of an increase in fatigability and vague generalized aches and pains. The aftermath of marihuana intoxication resembles an alcoholic "hangover." However, in contrast to alcoholics, marihuana users do not continue their indulgence beyond the point of euphoria, and soon learn to avoid becoming ill by remaining at a pleasurable distance from their maximum capacity for the drug. It may be mentioned that marihuana is no more aphrodisiac than is alcohol. . . .

Marihuana differs from the opium derivatives in that it does not give rise to a biological or physiological dependence. Discontinuance of the drug after its prolonged use does not result in withdrawal symptoms. The psychic habituation to marihuana is not as strong as to tobacco or alcohol. Use of marihuana over a long period of time may conduce to ingestion of progressively larger amounts merely through accessibility and familiarity. This increment however does not give rise to a more intense pleasurable experience. Thus a person experiencing pleasure with two marihuana cigarettes does not achieve any greater pleasure with six cigarettes, though he may indulge in them. . . .

Surprising Conclusions

In conclusion it is worthy of note that marijuana is probably taken by its users for the purpose of producing sensations comparable to those produced by alcohol. It causes a lowering of inhibitions comparable to that elicited by alcohol in a blood concentration of 2–3 mg. per cent. The user may speak and act more freely, is inclined to day-dreaming, and experiences a feeling of calm and pleasurable relaxation.

Marihuana, by virtue of its property of lowering inhibitions, accentuates all traits of personality, both those harmful and those beneficial. It does not impel its user to take spontaneous action, but may make his response to stimuli more emphatic than it normally would be. Increasingly larger doses of marihuana are not necessary in order that the long-term user may capture the original degree of pleasure.

Marihuana, like alcohol, does not alter the basic personality, but by relaxing inhibitions may permit antisocial tendencies formerly suppressed to come to the fore. Marihuana does not of itself give rise to anti-social behavior.

There is no evidence to suggest that the continued use of marihuana is a stepping-stone to the use of opiates. Prolonged use of the drug does not lead to physical, mental or moral degeneration, nor have we observed any permanent deleterious effects from its continued use. Quite the contrary, marihuana and its derivatives and allied synthetics have potentially valuable therapeutic applications which merit future investigation.

A Critique of Punitive Legislation

New York Academy of Medicine

In the years following World War II, the American media could once again turn its attention to domestic affairs, particularly rumors about unprecedented marijuana use among the country's youth. The surge of newspaper and magazine articles on the subject caught the attention of Senator Hale Boggs, a Democrat from Louisiana. Capitalizing on a renewed atmosphere of paranoia in the country, Boggs appeared before Congress with the only plan he believed would work: harsher penalties for drug offenders. Despite strong opposition, Boggs and others were able to persuade Congress that marijuana was a dangerous drug in part because it acted as a "gateway" that led users to try harder substances, such as heroin and cocaine. Congress passed the Boggs Act in 1951. It called for mandatory federal prison sentences for users and sellers of narcotics, including marijuana. The penalties were two to five years for the first offense, five to ten years for the second, and ten to twenty for the third. States responded to the new legislation by passing "Little Boggs Acts," which called for mandatory minimum state sentences to match those on the federal level. The following is an excerpt from a report by the Committee on Public Health of the New York Academy of Medicine, which was asked in 1955 to comment on the new punitive trend in drug enforcement laws. The academy concludes that the drug problem is severe in the United States but that the government's strategy of harsher penalties is not easing the addiction epidemic. The authors suggest a new approach to the drug war—

New York Academy of Medicine, "Report on Drug Addiction," *Bulletin of the New York Academy of Medicine*, vol. 31, 1955, pp. 601–607.

one that focuses on preventing the creation of new addicts and rehabilitating those who are already addicted.

From its appraisal of developments under the present punitive approach to the problem of drug addiction, it is the Academy's belief that the following conclusions are justified:

The illicit drug traffic still persists and it prevails in an even more sinister form since it now [in 1955] enslaves many youths.

Twenty-five years of the present laws have not accomplished to an unequivocal extent: suppression of illicit drug traffic; prevention of the spread of drug addiction.

The punitive approach is no deterrent to the non-addict dealer or to the addict. The threat of stiff penalties in the form of jail sentences has not prevented the non-addict dealer or the addict from taking the risk. Furthermore, the serving of sentences in jail has not proved the solution of drug addiction. For one thing, the record of repeat jail sentences for addicts is so large that the procedure has been called "the revolving door policy." For another, confinement in jails succeeds in thoroughly instructing in the ways of the underworld those addicts who had not yet engaged in criminal activity. Particularly in the case of young addicts the jail sentence is a dangerous approach to a medical problem. During incarceration the young addict, who had perhaps not even finished school because of his subjection to narcotics, learns from other prisoners not a skill with which he can support himself, but how to get along without working at all, even less desirable ways of maintaining his drug habit, and a complete course in drug addiction. It has been demonstrated that a jail sentence does nothing to help the addict recover from his addiction.

The Punitive Approach Is Ineffective

In view of the enormously magnified economic aspects of drug traffic, perhaps the punitive approach may not be the most effective way to bring about substantial reduction in drug addiction.

Under the law, most of the addicts are regarded as criminals rather than sick persons.

The present Federal regulations control the practice of medicine in relation to drug addiction to such an extent, and so look upon the physician as a potential criminal, that he prefers not to include the treatment of drug addiction in his practice.

Drug addiction is a more serious and difficult social and medical problem when it affects youths than older persons.

Judged by the criteria of abstinence from narcotics and, of accession to a gainful occupation in society, the rehabilitation of the drug addict in our present state of knowledge is a highly expensive, exceedingly slow and prolonged procedure necessitating repetitive efforts.

As a means of stamping out drug addiction, prevention remains the most practical and essential step. The crux of any program aimed to rid society of drug addiction is to stop the formation of new addicts. The program of the past has also been inadequate in two approaches which hold promise of contributing to the diminution of drug addiction: research and education. . . .

The Addict Should Be Treated as a Patient

The objective is to stamp out drug addiction as completely as possible. The crux of this objective is to diminish the number of individuals becoming newly addicted. The natural decrease with time in the number of existing addicts must not be overbalanced by the formation of new addicts at a more rapid rate. Indeed, if the objective of little or no addiction is to be achieved, there must be little or no formation of new addicts. Furthermore, whatever the policy adopted to abolish new addiction, there still remains the responsibility for those presently addicted. Concurrently with the attempt to stop the formation of new addicts, efforts should be directed to rehabilitate as many presently addicted persons as is possible. As a second objective such efforts would not only reduce the prevalence but would also contribute to stopping the spread of addiction. Finally, medical supervision should be provided for individuals already addicted to narcotic drugs who are resistant to rehabilitation.

The Academy proposes a six-point program to achieve these objectives. It should be emphasized that all measures are to be instituted, not just one.

1. There should be a change in attitude toward the addict. He is a sick person, not a criminal. That he may commit criminal acts to maintain his drug supply is recognized; but it is unjust to consider him criminal simply because he uses narcotic drugs.

2. The Academy believes that the most effective way to eradicate drug addiction is to take the profit out of the illicit drug traffic. The causes of addiction are cited as: maladjustment; underprivilege; broken home; poverty. Such conditions may well be contributory factors, but they are not of themselves the prime cause. Rather, profit looms large as the principal factor. . . .

Prospective users are furnished drugs by the "pusher" until addiction occurs. But once this has taken place, the addict is required to pay for every dose and thus a life of slavery begins. Therefore, the formation of new addicts is principally the result of commercial exploitation. Contained in the preamble of the Payne Bill[1] is the assertion: "Illicit traffic in narcotic drugs for profit are the primary and sustaining sources of addiction. . . . [sic]" If all profit were removed from dealings in narcotic drugs, there would be no incentive in giving away these drugs in an attempt to addict others.

The addict should be able to obtain his drugs at low cost under Federal control, in conjunction with efforts to have him

---

1. The Payne Bill of 1955 proposed amendments to various narcotics laws. Its provisions included transferring the Bureau of Narcotics from the Treasury Department to the Department of Justice, expanding facilities for the care and rehabilitation of drug addicts, and stiffer penalties for violation of narcotic laws. The bill was not passed.

undergo withdrawal. Under this plan, these addicts, as sick persons, would apply for medical care and supervision. Criminal acts would no longer be necessary in order to obtain a supply of drugs and there would be no incentive to create new addicts. Agents and black markets would disappear from lack of patronage. Since about eighty-five per cent of the "pushers" on the streets are said to be addicts, they would be glad to forego this dangerous occupation if they were furnished with their needed drug. Thus the bulk of the traffic would substantially disappear. By its very nature this traffic requires many agents scattered in diffuse neighborhoods. If a few un-addicted "pushers" were all that remained to carry on the trade, they would present a lesser problem for apprehension by the police.

The Importance of Rehabilitation

3. An integral part of the program would be medical supervision of existing addicts, with vigorous efforts toward their rehabilitation. No particular philosophy of stamping out drug addiction and traffic has an exclusive proprietary of rehabilition. Whatever the method it must include a plan and operation to rehabilitate the existing addict. This objective carries three parts: 1) persuasion of the addict to undergo treatment and rehabilitation; 2) appraisal of the methods of treatment and their success; 3) supervision of addicts who were resistant to undergoing treatment or refractory to treatment.

By a change in social attitude which would regard them as sick persons, and by relieving them of the economic oppression of attempting to obtain their supply of drug at an exorbitant price, it will be possible to reach existing addicts in an orderly dignified way, not as probationed persons or sentenced criminals. They would come under supervision in the interest of health, not because of entanglement with the law. Thereafter, on a larger scale and in a humanitarian atmosphere, there would be opportunity to apply persuasion to undergo rehabilitation. It is reasonable to expect that more might accept the opportunity.

It is a temptation to think of addicts as a homogeneous group, whereas all that they have in common is their addiction. They differ in age, personality, constitution, social and cultural environment, and length of time of addiction. Each addict is therefore an individual therapeutic problem. Present methods to convert addicts into abstainers have comprised removal of the drug and then institution of rehabilitative measures. Physical dependence on drugs can be removed by the withdrawal treatment. The mental and emotional fixations, however, are to be overcome only through the individual's own efforts and desires. Psychotherapy cannot be forced upon him with any hope of lasting benefit. Rehabilitation of severely addicted individuals to the point where they abstain from drugs for the remainder of their lives has been shown to be an extremely slow process with an equally slow rate of success. The present therapeutic regimen has suffered from premature termination of support to the patient. There is a need to maintain continuing contact with recovered addicts so that they may be helped in resisting the return to use of a drug in stress situations. A counselling service for them is urgently needed. . . .

The Suggested Role of the Law

4. It is proposed that there be no relaxation in the efforts toward complete and permanent elimination of the supply of illegal narcotic drugs and that provisions for suppression of illegal traffic be retained. It is the Academy's belief that the suggested plan to remove the profit would diminish illicit traffic. Whatever illicit operations were left after its application should be vigorously eradicated by appropriate laws, their enforcement, and provision for suitable penalties. Here illicit traffic should be re-defined to allow provision of drugs to addicts under medical supervision and treatment. This procedure

should be surrounded by suitable safeguards. If anyone receiving drugs under the supportive plan should be found attempting to receive or to be receiving supplies from more than one clinic or from an illicit market, or if he be found attempting to sell or actually selling any of his supply to another person, he should be liable to commitment to a hospital with attempted rehabilitation. Thus he should be controlled as a sick person, not as a criminal.

Initially, it would be essential to provide the trained staff necessary to apprehend the peddlers, wholesalers and importers. It goes without saying that this group will not give up its lucrative business without a struggle. But a dearth of drug users, combined with severe penalties for dealing in narcotics, could be expected to put an end to the illicit drug traffic within a relatively short time.

It should be emphasized that the law should draw a distinction between the addict and non-addict in its provision. The convicted non-addict trafficker should feel its full force.

5. Adolescent addicts are reported to have said that they would not have taken drugs in the first place if they had known that they were going to become addicted. Such statements of youth are a strong argument for a good educational program for young people. The adult user, too, reports that he did not know the dangers of narcotic drugs when he began their use. If such reports are correct, it would appear that an educational program for adults as well as for adolescents is needed.

Combined with the medical care of narcotic addicts and severe penalties for trafficking in drugs, there should be an adequate program of education for adults, teachers and youth. By means of all education media, including radio, television, the public press, forum, lecture, books and pamphlets, there should be a concerted effort at informing the public of the dangers of narcotic drugs. Furthermore, there should be impressed upon the population the need to treat addicts, to apprehend illicit drug dealers, and to avoid the use of such drugs except under medical supervision.

The Need for Continued Study

6. One of the great difficulties in planning for a medical approach in the care and supervision of addicts is the lack of accurate information on their number. So long as they are stamped as criminals that difficulty will exist. It is a merit of the medical approach that by adopting the proper attitude toward them, it should be possible to study the epidemiology of drug addiction and acquire information about the magnitude and pathogenesis of the disease.

By means of the records accumulated at the central agency, it would be possible to have at all times an accurate count of the known resistant addicts in the country. It would also be possible to know how many addicts were undergoing treatment for their illness and how many relapsed after a period of abstinence. Data on the length of abstinence from narcotic drugs and therefore on the success of various types of treatment would be obtainable. On the basis of such information, research could be focused more readily on the "why" of addiction and on improved methods of treatment. There seems little possibility of learning the "why" of addiction until narcotic addicts can be studied under conditions more nearly approximating normal existence than do those of a hospital, excellent though it may be.

So much has been stated about the relation of drug addiction and crime, particularly about the need for drugs leading to crime, that the Academy is moved to state that realistically it has no extravagant expectations that the proposed plan will completely eliminate crime. If a person was a criminal before he became a drug addict, it is not necessarily to be expected that he will cease to follow his predilections for crime just because he no longer is an addict. Perhaps it is fair to state that crime arising from the need for drugs may diminish; but criminal acts committed for other reasons may not decrease.

It is the opinion of the Academy that this program, taken in its entirety, is a reasonable and humane approach to the solution of drug addiction. It must be frankly admitted that there is no ideal or perfect solution. Of the two possible approaches to the solution of the problem, the punitive as against the medical, it becomes a matter of judgment as to which gives the more promise of effectiveness and contains fewer points of vulnerability. In judging between them the Academy believes that the evidence is preponderantly in favor of its proposed program as the more promising means of ridding the nation of drug addiction.

CHAPTER THREE

The Marijuana Controversy in the 1960s and 1970s

Marijuana Gains Acceptance

Richard J. Bonnie and Charles H. Whitebread II

In this excerpt from their book on America's history of marijuana prohibition, two professors of law, Richard J. Bonnie and Charles H. Whitebread II, explain how the social consensus on marijuana began to dissolve during the 1960s. Marijuana's status as a dangerous narcotic and its association with criminal behavior and minority communities had created a general attitude of intolerance during the first half of the twentieth century. The cultural climate of the 1960s changed the perceptions of marijuana and its users, however. The civil rights movement, the fight for free speech, and widespread disapproval of the Vietnam War created an environment of protest and skepticism. In turn, some people began to question marijuana's purported dangers, and the drug became more commonly accepted. The average American had to admit that marijuana was now infiltrating mainstream culture. As America's prisons overflowed with recreational users, many wondered whether the strict laws against cannabis were doing more harm to society than good. However, the U.S. government maintained its enforcement of the drug, and a new, negative stereotype of the marijuana user replaced the old. He or she was no longer a Mexican or black youth prone to random violence, but a lazy, maladjusted, politically radical hippie. Nonetheless, marijuana had permeated all ranks of society by the late 1960s, and the government had no choice but to reconsider its strategy and relax its laws. In 1969 the U.S. Supreme Court ruled the 1937

Marihuana Tax Act unconstitutional. Once Richard Nixon took office in 1969, however, a new "war on drugs" began.

For fifty years a latent social consensus supported the nation's marihuana laws. This marihuana consensus was buttressed by a number of ideological and descriptive propositions. The belief that marihuana was a "narcotic" drug was of primary importance. The statutory definitions of marihuana in most states codified this, especially after the passage of the Uniform Act.[1] In other states and in federal legislation, penalty provisions were based upon it. In legal status and in the legislative mind, marihuana was indistinguishable from the opiates and cocaine.

Aspects of the Consensus

Marihuana prohibition rested in large part on the essential premise of the narcotics policy that use inevitably became abuse. The view that narcotics users were incapable of moderation was reflected in the overwhelming urge to refer to marihuana users as "addicts" and to postulate a strong psychological compulsion for use even if no physiological compulsion existed. There was also a predisposition to attribute other dysfunctional effects to marihuana. Policy makers were inclined to look for high incidences of mental deterioration, psychosis, and violent crime.

Another essential condition of the marihuana consensus was the demography of that portion of the population using it. Because it was used primarily by insulated ethnic minorities, Mexicans and blacks, the drug was always associated with the lowest levels of the socioeconomic structure. This had several important consequences. First, since the user populations were associated in the public mind with crime, idleness, and

1. The Uniform State Narcotic Drug Act of 1927–1937 was endorsed by the Federal Bureau of Narcotics as an alternative to federal legislation. It made marijuana a "narcotic" by state law.

other antisocial behavior, a causal relationship between marihuana and such behavior seemed evident. Second, since these
insulated minorities had no access to the policy-making and
public opinion processes, hypotheses supporting this consensus went unchallenged. Sharing the basic public policy predisposition, the medical and scientific communities felt no particular need to study the drug and its effects, especially after
cannabis was removed from the U.S. pharmacopoeia. The little research which was conducted tended to undercut prevailing beliefs, but these inconsistencies remained unpublicized
because there was no constituency interested in revealing
them. The narcotics bureaucracy was also, of course, inclined
to suppress them.

Final support for the marihuana consensus came from ideological factors reflected in American public policy during the
first six decades of [the twentieth] century. Resting on society's
interest in individual productivity and its preference for cultural homogeneity was a legislative tendency to inhibit any
personal behavior thought to be incompatible with society's
best interests. Two world wars, the depression, several reces-
sions, the Korean conflict, and a cold war, kept the nation on
the defensive. There was little tolerance for personal deviance.
The notion that there was a sphere of personal activity im-
mune from governmental scrutiny lost its constitutional foot-
ing. Legislatures continually sought to compel sexual, sensual,
and even intellectual orthodoxy. As increased geographic mobility, institutional growth, and mass communications gradually loosened the capacities of nonlegal institutions—the family, church, schools—to regulate behavior, society relied more
and more on the legal system, and the criminal law in particular, to symbolize and enforce the dominant order.

A New Class of Users

Beginning in the mid-sixties, the marihuana consensus evap-
orated, as each of its essential supports wobbled and fell away.

The drug's sudden attraction to the nation's university population was of primary importance. Although marihuana arrests and seizures had hit their all-time low point in 1960, by 1967 use of the drug was associated in the public mind with life on the campus. This new class of users, regardless of its size, had direct access to the public opinion process because it was drawn from the middle and upper socioeconomic brackets. As a result, this new use pattern incited a broad social awareness of the drug and awakened in the scientific and medical communities a new interest in research.

It is difficult to account entirely for this new interest in marihuana and to pinpoint exactly when it began. In all likelihood marihuana use may have been the most visible by-product of the merger of several different social and political movements in the mid-sixties. Perhaps the most specific of these was the national publicity given the LSD experimentation at Harvard University by Drs. [of psychology Timothy] Leary and [Richard] Alpert in 1963. As a growing segment of the academic fringe began to preach consciousness-expansion, student attention and curiosity in the Northeast became focused on drugs and drug use.

At the same time, the so-called psychedelic movement was launched on the West Coast, particularly in the San Francisco area. . . . As the [San Francisco] Haight-Asbury scene and the West Coast drug culture attracted interest in the press, student curiosity across the country was aroused, as was that of the intellectual avant-garde in [New York City's] Greenwich Village and similar urban communities.

Marihuana Is Different from Opiates and Cocaine

A much more pervasive social development influencing the interest in marihuana was a general loosening of restraints imposed by the legal system on behavior with "moral" overtones. Beginning with the widely acclaimed civil rights movement of the early 1960s, proceeding through the free speech movement, the antiwar movement, and the ecology movement, the decade was characterized by protest and civil disobedience. [Civil rights leader] Martin Luther King's appeal to the higher moral law and the righteousness of his cause made a deep impression on the national conscience, piercing most deeply the souls of the country's youth. The civil rights movement weakened the moral force of the law as an institution by illustrating the evil which could be codified by secular authorities. This tendency was exacerbated, particularly among those in college, by the Vietnam escalation, which began in 1965. Disobedience of the marihuana laws may have been a convenient offspring of the protest attitude. Marihuana, of course, was ready-made for such a symbolic use, having been miscast in the past and being so easily aligned against the establishment's own alcohol.

Whatever its genesis, the change in use patterns immediately affected a number of conditions upon which the marihuana consensus rested. Most obvious was the challenge to the drug's classification as a narcotic. The revelation that marihuana was substantially *different* from the opiates and cocaine made a major impact on public attitudes. The substitution of other labels such as "dangerous drug" or "hallucinogen" did not negate this impact; nor did the initial judicial conclusions that the legislature could legitimately classify marihuana as a "narcotic" even though it was not technically accurate to do so. . . .

The causal relationships between marihuana and crime, idleness, and incapacitation were now more difficult to maintain. The new users were not "criminals" or social outcasts. They were sons and daughters of the middle and upper classes. In short, when the consensus against marihuana lost its sociological support, it immediately lost its scientific support as well.

Ideological Opposition

The continued vitality of its ideological support had also become debatable. Whereas society formerly imposed severe restraints on the individual's personal and social conduct in order to reap the benefits of his economic and political independence, another view was winning an increasing number of adherents. Under this view economic and political institutions have become increasingly omnipotent; the individual is increasingly dependent on the system rather than the system being dependent on him. Increasing numbers of individuals view themselves as cogs in the massive, impersonal, technological machine, the controls for which are beyond their grasp. Consequently, it is argued, a higher value must be placed on personal fulfillment in the noneconomic, nonpolitical sphere. A new emphasis must be placed on personal identity and the individualized, deinstitutionalized pursuit of happiness. Concurrently, as economic productivity demands less of each individual's time and energy, and the workweek continues to shorten, a leisure ethic is emerging. From the perspective of productivity, the argument goes, society has less and less economic interest in what the individual does with his leisure time.

During the mid-sixties this ideological development was manifested in laws and judicial decisions upholding the individual's right to differ—intellectually, spiritually, socially, and sensually. Concurrently, a renascent emphasis on individual privacy appeared. As an incredibly sophisticated technology continually expanded society's control over the individual, he began to insist that the wall around his private life be fortified. The courts responded, proscribing official snooping and invalidating laws interfering with familial decision-making—abortion, contraception, miscegenation—and with private sexual conduct.

A related trend, well underway during the sixties, was deemphasis of the criminal law as a means of social control. Increasing numbers of legal scholars and social scientists were beginning to indict the process of "overcriminalization" under which the sphere of criminal conduct had been too broadly drawn. Of particular interest are offenses committed in private, by consenting individuals, such as drug offenses. The view that the criminal law was not the only, or even the best, way for society to express its disapproval of certain behavior was certainly a notion foreign to early twentieth-century policy makers.

A new class of users, revived scientific interest and debate, lively public interest, and fundamental ideological crosscurrents all combined to undermine the marihuana consensus in the mid-sixties. This is not to say, however, that the law was no longer defensible or defended—only that conflict replaced consensus. For the first time in its fifty-year history, marihuana prohibition encountered an operating public opinion process.

Fear of the Counterculture

A public policy so deeply rooted as marihuana prohibition does not wither away in the heat of debate, especially when it is embodied in criminal law and is thus presumed to circumscribe socially harmful and immoral activity. In this case the immediate tendency was to retrench and lash out at marihuana use. The uneasiness with which the dominant social order viewed the political and racial disruption of the mid-sixties contributed to this reaction. Violent demonstrations and urban riots threatened to tear the society apart physically, while an emerging "hippie" counterculture threatened to do so spiritually by overtly rejecting the prevailing value system and by "dropping out" of society altogether.

Since it was associated with misguided young, marihuana easily became a symbol of these wider social conflicts. A new stereotype of the marihuana user was substituted for the old. From the establishment's side, defense of marihuana prohibition and enforcement of the law was one way to assert the vitality and superiority of the dominant system and thereby extirpate the "permissivists" and "revolutionaries" who aimed to topple that system. Not surprisingly, the marihuana laws were often used selectively as a vehicle for removing radical irritants from the body politic and lazy hippies from the streets.

But the symbolism of the marihuana prohibition was Janus-faced. As we have suggested, marihuana-smoking was an attractive way for the alienated counterculture to taunt the establishment and flout its laws. For the New Left,[2] the drug's illegal status—which put large numbers of young people on the wrong side of the criminal law—was a useful recruiting agent. Some radical leaders went so far as to *oppose* reduction in penalties for marihuana possession because they felt severe penalties aided their recruiting efforts by making marihuana users outraged against the society that overreacted so strongly to a nonexistent danger. . . .

Law Enforcement Intensifies

The official retrenchment characterizing the 1965–68 period was led by the law enforcement community. Official propaganda shifted its emphasis away from concerns engendered by the old user population to those associated with the new. The FBN [Federal Bureau of Narcotics] continued to propagate the crime thesis—complete with the kind of anecdotal support used in the old days—but most official spokesmen characterized the problem in terms of public health rather than public safety. The emerging view regarded the marihuana user as a troubled, emotionally unstable individual. Psychological dependence, amotivation, alienation, and an inevitable tendency to use other drugs became the cornerstone of official doctrine.

Within the medical community, increasing numbers of physicians and public health experts were becoming uncomfortable with the official line. But once marihuana became politicized, authoritative medical spokesmen were aware that their statements would be wielded in the rhetorical battle; they therefore employed extreme caution, emphasizing what might be true as well as what was. . . .

Medical experts generally distinguish between experimental and chronic use, between use and "abuse." For example, the

2. The New Left is a term for the generation of Americans who came of age in the 1960s and became involved in struggles against social injustices.

AMA [American Medical Association] Council on Mental Health and Committee on Alcoholism and Drug Dependence emphasized that American marihuana use was generally experimental or intermittent use of weak cannabis preparations, and that the medical hazard involved in this situation is low compared to that associated with chronic heavy use. Yet, this distinction was generally omitted in dissemination to the public by FBN spokesmen who continually cited both the WHO and AMA reports in support of more drastic propositions. Well into 1968 the FBN held firm against the "permissivist" onslaught, . . . insisting that marihuana was a "highly dangerous substance with inherent physical dangers" and maintaining that marihuana users should continue to be felons.

In any event, a common theme within both the medical and law enforcement communities was that marihuana-smoking was a chemical cop-out, suggestive, at least, of underlying psychological instability. For example, one medical expert noted that in the West, marihuana seems to "possess a particular attraction for certain psychologically and socially maladjusted persons who have difficulty conforming to usual social norms.". . .

Researchers Versus the Government

Meanwhile, in the laboratories and on the campuses medical researchers were gradually permitted to seek answers to the basic scientific questions. This effort was methodologically facilitated in 1966 when $\Delta 9$THC [delta-9-tetrahydrocannabinol], the active principle in cannabis, was synthesized, and then in 1967 when its pharmacological effects were demonstrated. Young researchers like Andrew Weil of Harvard were anxious to perform clinical human studies, and the National Institute of Mental Health [NIMH] was inundated with requests to approve and fund marihuana research. Apart from pharmacological research, social scientists unleashed an entire arsenal of questionnaires on a new social entity: the "marihuana user."

Any new research had an interested audience and, depending on its policy implications, immediate critics.

Having defaulted for forty years, the scientific community no longer had the luxury of time and precision. The public wanted answers, and official spokesmen wanted the right ones. The FBN chief counsel made this quite clear in 1968:

> The real damage being done in this crisis of confidence is that some scholarly men are more willing to attack the marihuana controls than to justify them: that these persons are more concerned with deriding the public officials who are charged with enforcing the laws than in helping them prevent drug abuse; and that they are more interested in rationalizing the use of marihuana than in presenting reasons for controlling it.

There was thus an inherent conflict in the interests of researchers and the interests of the government. This collision was most intense during 1967–68 when the FBN and NIMH struggled to develop procedures for selecting the "right" research applications, thereby demonstrating the government's interest in seeking the truth while minimizing the risk of embarrassing results. . . .

Unwavering Legislation

Law enforcement officials were not stemming the tide alone. Legislators would not budge, and the courts had no trouble "presenting reasons for controlling" marihuana when the prohibition was challenged. In fact, the retrenchment period is best exemplified by a twelve-day evidentiary hearing held before a Massachusetts Superior Court judge on the question of whether or not marihuana was rationally classified as a narcotic. In defense of two Philadelphia youngsters charged with possession, conspiracy, and possession with intent to sell, Attorney Joseph S. Oteri challenged the constitutionality of the Massachusetts law, parading numerous scientific witnesses before the bench. With the close cooperation of the FBN, the prosecution solicited a similar array of expert witnesses in support of the law. The challenge failed; in the end, the presence of Science on the witness stand made absolutely no difference. . . .

Another example of the fate of official dissent occurred on the state level. In 1966 the California legislature launched a major effort to reform its criminal code. Following tradition, the legislature relied on the legal academic community for the basic drafting, appointing six reporters to assist the Joint Legislative Committee to Revise the Penal Code. One of these reporters was John Kaplan, professor of law at Stanford Law School and a former assistant U.S. Attorney. As reporter he devoted much of his energy to the drug laws and the marihuana laws in particular. After more than two years of study and soul-searching, the reporters unanimously circulated a preliminary draft on marihuana in early 1969, recommending the withdrawal of the criminal penalty from possession for personal use. Shortly thereafter the Joint Legislative Committee fired the six reporters and replaced them with a prosecutor from the attorney general's office. After his dismissal, Professor Kaplan gathered the available information and published it, [in *Marijuana: The New Prohibition*] appealing in his word, to a "tribunal of higher resort."

The Continued Spread of Marihuana

While the establishment symbolized its concern about the young generation by defending the marihuana laws, use of the drug nonetheless continued to spread. As more novice marihuana users reported no ill effects from its use, more students tried it, and in turn those who used it and enjoyed the drug began to "turn on" those who had not. By 1970 some campuses reported that over 70 percent of the student body were users. Most observers and surveys estimated that about 50 percent of the nation's college population had tried marihuana. Meanwhile, use of the drug was spreading beyond students to the young professional classes in the cities and later to blue-collar youths. Marihuana became popular with many soldiers because the drug was readily available and widely used in Vietnam. On their return they introduced the practice to still wider segments of the population.

During the last few years of the sixties, then, marihuana use became less identified with any particular class or age. Dipping further into the teenage population and touching increasing numbers of the twenty-five to thirty-five-year-old group, experimental and recreational use of the drug touched all classes of society. By 1970 the *Wall Street Journal* found substantial marihuana use among young professionals and considerable evidence of marihuana use on the job in the New York City area.

As this trend continued, it became a popular sport to try to estimate the total incidence of use among Americans. Dr. Stanley F. Yolles, former director of the National Institute of Mental Health, testifying before a Senate subcommittee in 1969, said: "A conservative estimate of persons in the United States, both juveniles and adults, who have used marihuana at least once, is about eight million. And may be as high as twelve million people." Other estimates in the late 1960s ran as high as twenty-five million users. Although all the polls suffered from methodological flaws, it was generally accepted that use continued to increase into the seventies.

Meanwhile, of course, marihuana-smoking had become the most widely committed crime in America, with the possible exception of speeding on the highways. . . . It has been estimated that approximately 200,000 persons were arrested for possession of marihuana in 1970.

Marihuana-smoking was no longer associated entirely with radical politics and the hippie lifestyle. In fact, both these social phenomena had probably declined after 1968, and the public anxiety that had characterized the retrenchment period had also receded. Instead, public attention had been turned increasingly to the legal consequences of marihuana use. In September 1970, for example, *Newsweek* headlined its cover story with the question "Marihuana: Time to Change the Law?" Despite the retrenchment rhetoric, uncertainty—about the effects of the drug, and particularly about the propriety of prosecuting and incarcerating its users—now dominated public opinion. Information regarding the harmfulness of marihuana was now less important than information regarding the harmfulness—or costs—of the marihuana laws. The public began to hear a lot about misallocation of enforcement resources, arbitrary prosecution, questionable police practices, and disrespect for law. Instances of political pot prosecutions and convictions were documented in the press. One of the most notorious was the thirty-year sentence meted out by a Texas court to black militant Lee Otis Johnson for giving one joint to an undercover agent. At the time of his conviction in 1968, Johnson headed the Houston chapter of the Student Nonviolent Coordinating Committee (SNCC). His conviction was subsequently reversed in 1972 by a federal district court.

Opponents of the marihuana laws also argued that it was the marihuana *laws*, not marihuana itself, which could lead to "harder stuff" by compelling the marihuana user to secure his drug in an illicit marketplace. Most potent, however, was the challengers' contention that no possible harmful drug effect could justify the social cost of criminalizing the otherwise law-abiding young. Anthropologist Margaret Mead contended [in the *New York Times* in October 1971] that marihuana prohibition was "damaging our country, our laws and the relations between young and old." An otherwise cautious AMA expert committee statement [that appeared in the *Journal of the American Medical Association*] in 1968 pleaded for differential legal approaches for "the occasional user, the frequent user, the chronic user, the person sharing his drug with another, and the dealer who sells for profit." Of "particular concern," the AMA experts emphasized, "is the youthful experimenter who, by incurring a criminal record through a single thoughtless act, places his future career in jeopardy. The lives of many young people are being needlessly damaged."

The retreat had begun. The law enforcement community began to compromise the law, and the legislatures began to change it. The medical community gradually became willing to state the facts, abandoning the uneasy defensiveness of the re-trenchment period. The underlying policy issues still remained unresolved, but the waiting period was over.

The Debate over Whether Marijuana Causes Apathy

Larry "Ratso" Sloman

Larry "Ratso" Sloman was born in New York City in 1948. After working a number of odd jobs, he finally landed a position in 1979 as editor in chief of the promarijuana magazine *High Times*. That same year, he published *On the Road with Bob Dylan: Rolling with the Thunder* and *Reefer Madness: The History of Marijuana in America*. The latter garnered national attention for its candid and often amusing portrait of the American marijuana culture. In the following excerpt from his book, Sloman explores a popular myth that arose in the seventies about marijuana's long-term effects: "the amotivational syndrome." According to some, people who smoke marijuana stop caring about their goals and drop off into the ranks of the unproductive and apathetic. Knowing quite a few successful pot smokers himself, Sloman doubted the validity of the "syndrome." In an attempt to address this paradox—as well as the rumor that marijuana decreases verbal and intellectual skills—he journeys to a supposedly typical middle-class home in Westchester, New York, where three entrepreneurial couples who use marijuana wait to be interviewed. He describes an evening of pot-induced conversation with Barbara S. and her friends, the new breed of established and successful marijuana smokers. Barbara and her friends claim that marijuana makes them more creative in their jobs, helps them to focus, and deepens their sense of self-awareness. Although they do admit that marijuana causes some absentmindedness and even a bit of "antimotivation," they still believe that the benefits of smoking marijuana far outweigh the consequences. Larry Sloman is also the author of *Steal This Dream: Abbie Hoffman and the Countercultural Revolution in America*.

Barbara, an amiable, attractive woman in her mid-thirties, managed the career of one of America's most popular schlock artists, a woman whose prints could be had at most department stores across the country. Most of her friends were also young professionals, and besides their similarity in terms of class and occupation, they all shared a common interest in marijuana. They had all turned their back on liquor and had adopted the weed as their recreational drug of choice. [The author Larry] Sloman thought it would be fascinating to interview these young, ambitious middle-class potheads, so Barbara used the interview situation as an excuse to party. Barbara would have used almost anything as an excuse to party.

But Sloman had more than just an interview in mind. He was intrigued by one of the arguments that the anti-marijuana legions still used in their attempts to prevent the use of the substance. Basically, they argued that smoking pot leads to something called the "amotivational syndrome." According to this view, marijuana itself causes a certain brain syndrome marked by distortion of perceptions, impairment of judgment, diminished attention span, a difficulty with verbalization, and a loss of thought continuity. The user then becomes apathetic, disoriented and oftentimes depressed—in short, amotivated. This view had been promulgated most forcefully by Harold Kolansky and William Moore, two Philadelphia psychiatrists who stirred tremendous controversy in the early seventies with a few journal articles outlining this syndrome.

But Sloman had always perceived this issue as a value-laden one. It seemed that the "syndrome" Kolansky and Moore were describing emerged from a set of values that pot smokers in the sixties for the most part shared. When smoking pot was seen as a radical act, as a means of attaining a consciousness that helped one to "see" through the "lies" of the power structure, users exhibited behavior that to a member of the power structure (or one sympathetic to that view) would appear to be amotivational. In other words, to understand this concept, we must define "motivation," and to most of these researchers, "motivation" was any act that would be consistent with attaining status in a competitive, capitalistic society. Conversely, you were "amotivated," and therefore "sick," if you sat around all day smoking pot, listening to music, watching your plants grow, basically having a good time. Having a good time, of course, is not consistent with attaining status in a competitive, capitalistic society.

A New Breed of Pot Smokers

But tonight, Sloman and [his friends] the Cusimanos would encounter a new breed of pot smokers, users who would send Kolansky and Moore scurrying back to their couches in an attempt to explain away their presence. Barbara and her friends smoked grass regularly and enjoyed it enormously. However, they also had grandiose ambitions; they wanted to make oodles and oodles of money, garner a tremendous amount of prestige, work very hard at what it was that they did, and enjoy the fruits of their labors through the benefits of a highly developed consumer society. They were the New Hedonists, and their story was what Sloman was after.

Barbara answered the door and ushered the visitors in, introducing them to Eric and Mary, a couple from Manhattan who had arrived early. Eric was a manufacturer of nuts and screws, and Mary, his wife, was a budding interior decorator. They were both in their mid-thirties and well groomed. Cusimano self-consciously touched his torn blue Banlon shirt.

"Here, why don't you start on this?" Ira, Barbara's husband, threw a handful of well-rolled joints onto the coffee table. "There's more after that's finished." In the next room, the children were engaged in loud play.

"Oh god, I want the kids to go to sleep." Mary looked a bit uptight.

"Don't worry." Sloman showed how easy it was to palm a joint.

"No, no," Mary corrected. "I want them to go to sleep before they start smoking all the other things. With the big pipes going around."

Barbara, who had been working on the food in the kitchen, came in. "You know what?" she said in her distinctive nasal tones. "I need a joint myself. I'm really much too straight to be alive. Thank you. Back to my kitchen duties."

But the doorbell interrupted, and Barbara admitted two more couples, all about the same age and all dressed similarly to Barbara and the others present. "Close the door," Barbara was directing traffic, ushering the newcomers in. "Give them joints immediately, please.". . .

Sloman began setting up his recorder, and then he set down the ground rules for the interview. They could talk about anything they wanted; it would be an informal chat. But for the purposes of the transcriber, everyone would in turn at first give his or her name, occupation, age and how many years a smoker. To allay their fears, the participants were allowed to make up names, which about one-quarter of the group chose to do. One by one, they went around the room.

"This is ridiculous," Irma, who chose to be called Petunia, scoffed. "This sounds like we're on David Susskind [host of his own talk show from 1967–1986]."

"Do you talk about how it progressed from when you started out, or do you talk about right now?" Barbara worried as she brought in the third variety of dip for the snacks on the coffee table.

"You can do anything. It's open-ended," Sloman reassured her.

Turning On to Pot

"I'll tell you how we started," Ira, who in his fantasies chose Clyde as his nom de pot [a word play on "nom de plume" or pen name], began. "For many years when we were younger there was a bunch of people we always went out with. Three or four couples. Constantly. Until we got married and after a while we found they were going out but they weren't asking us. We couldn't imagine what the reasons were. So we finally got them to the house and we asked them point-blank why they were going out and not asking us. They said they'd started smoking marijuana. They knew Barbara was dead set against it."

"I was like really moralistically off the wall about it," Barbara grinned sheepishly.

"Basically because she said it was against the law and she was afraid of getting busted," Ira continued. "After spending a good ten years with all these people, we stopped seeing them. Then we got into a new bunch of friends. It turned out that everybody we met had already smoked pot. I don't even remember who turned us on one night. We didn't even buy. We used to borrow."

"We'd borrow wherever we went." Barbara took a hit and passed a joint, only to find another one coming up on her left.

"Like two cigarettes a week or something," Ira remembered. "Then we started buying half ounces, then ounces, now we're up to three ounces at a time. It's still illegal, but I think that now Barbara finds everybody you speak to smokes marijuana. That's why she smokes constantly. She's a real head." Ira glanced proudly at his wife.

"I start to smoke as soon as I put my ass on the seat of the car when I close the office door," Barbara smiled. "I take out my dollar for the toll and my joint for the ride. As soon as I leave the office I'm shaking. I have even smoked before I went to work. When Ira drives me to work at nine in the morning, he's always smoking, so I smoke. I've done it at least half a dozen times, gone to work stoned. And I did the very biggest and most outrageous thing of my entire career one morning because I was stoned. I got the J.C. Penney's Mother's Day promotion because I was so stoned."

"You mean the idea came to you?" Sloman asked.

"We got it all and we did it. And that was because I went in stoned. But sometimes when I go in stoned I can't get my first telephone call made. I'll be talking to myself. I walked out of my office once on my way someplace and then I got there and said, 'What the hell am I here for?'" Barbara exploded into torrents of laughter, warm, infectious laughter that quickly spread around the semi-stoned room.

"When Barbara smokes she doesn't know what she's doing," Ira patiently explained. "She smoked this afternoon, walked into the bedroom, stood in there looking around, couldn't figure out what she was doing in there, and then realized she had gone in to get dressed. This goes on all the time. She'll start saying something and she'll forget what she was saying."

"I don't exactly like 100 percent of what it does to me," the hostess admitted. "I like 80 percent of what it does."

"What does it do for you?" Sloman inquired as he passed up a joint, to a lingering stare from Irma.

"It makes me understand where I'm at. I think thoughts so clearly and I get so far into myself or whatever I'm thinking about. If I get into a project at work, I get into that project. I mean I'm really into that project. Nothing's left unturned." Barbara smiled proudly. . . .

Their Smoking Habits

"Ira, do you work stoned?"

"I'll come up [to my home] during the day for three or four hours, and I'll smoke when I come up, but by the time I go down [to work] I'm never stoned. I never work on anybody stoned unless it's in the house, one of the kids or Barbara," Ira related.

"We don't care if *they* die," Barbara cracked.

"If I smoke during the day I might get a call and have to go into the office and adjust someone stoned because I have no choice. Sometimes I do better work that way," Ira smiled. "A lot of the practice of chiropractics is the feeling by touch. Bone displacement, just by feeling it. When I'm stoned my fingers are much more sensitive than when I'm not. I'm much more aware of what I'm feeling. I know exactly what's in the body, in the spine, so I know exactly what the bone looks like that I'm working on. But when I'm stoned I can picture the whole back with no skin on it better than when I'm not stoned."

"Yeah, when he gets straight he finds out he's really working on a skeleton," Fred quipped.

By now about ten joints had been consumed, and Ira got up and came back shortly with another handful, scattering them on the coffee table.

"So basically we're talking about a substance that promotes creativity, helps us think better, relaxes us, takes away pain, but the reality is it's still illegal. Do you feel that?" Sloman was sounding more and more like David Susskind.

"There used to be a time when you put the towel by the door," Eric remembered.

"Do any of you smoke in public?" Cusimano was curious. "Outdoors?"

"We did it in a restaurant one night." Carol smiled. "About forty of us at the Ground Round."

"We smoke in movies," her husband Steve added.

"We smoke on the beach and in the car," Ira related.

"Walking through Bloomingdale's—I've seen people do that," Carol recollected. "My sister walks down the street all the time smoking. We were at a bar mitzvah and the people at the next table were stoned."

"And the bar mitzvah boy was stoned," Fred added. . . .

Changes in Perception

Cusimano quickly changed the subject. "Has grass changed your perceptions? Made you a different person?"

"I think that it would have a tendency to change anybody's life who smoked it as an everyday thing." Barbara got serious for a rare moment. "I have found that it changes my perspective on just so many things that I have become that much more aware. I'm so much more introspective. You start touching yourself. You start getting into your own head. Who the hell ever knew the things that were—I never knew the things that were happening in my head. I had no idea."

"But you're an outgoing person," Fred interrupted. "You smoke grass and you maintain your posture as an outgoing person. Do you think someone who is shy and introverted who smokes grass suddenly as a result. . . ."

"You don't know what's going on inside when you're so extroverted," Barbara objected. "I could say things very easily to people, but I had no idea what was going on. It's the first time in my life when I started to smoke that I got in touch with my feelings. 'Cause your head starts to work. You could be in a totally unconscious state sometimes when you're straight. You can go through the day unaware. Grass has changed my whole life. I went in a certain direction. I've taken steps that were bolder than I might have done. I went through all kinds of trips with regard to having to work or not having to work, leaving your children. That's a heavy trip for a person to do. I think smoking is what really made me able to go through with it and understand it and come to terms with it better."

"Those are experiences that are between you and the marijuana as opposed to between you and your best friends?" Sloman probed.

"You know what? It's an experience of me and the marijuana. But what happens is I'll experience the thought and I have a dear friend who I can speak to and tell it to. And when I say it out loud and she throws it back at me . . . I know I've been through some heavy trips that I might have had to go to a shrink for to talk this stuff out. To get somebody to get it the hell out of me. It works on both levels. You by yourself and you being able to speak more freely."

"What a great concept, a marijuana friend," Sloman marveled.

"You get a chapter," Fred joked, and lit up a joint.

"Many times she gets into bed and she's ready to go to sleep and she turns on the light and starts writing on her pad because she's had an idea," Ira offered, nodding toward his wife.

"What kind of idea? For business?" Sloman posed.

Barbara nodded. "For business."

"What about poems? Stuff like that?"

"Are you kidding?" Barbara shrieked. "I see numbers, prints, colors, subject matter, picture frames. That's all I see, honey."

Everyone cracked up. "I think if you're stoned and you go to sleep you can get more into fantasy," Fred reported. . . .

Marijuana and Parenting

Barbara finished the last of the dip and looked anxiously around. "Do you think we should break for sandwiches now? Everybody's so hungry." Her hunger elicited laughs from the group.

"I want to ask one question," Fred broke in. "You touched on something before. I'd like to know how the other people in this room handle their children with grass."

Carol began laughing. "My mother called from Florida this morning, and the first words out of my six-year-old were, 'Gee, Mommy's been smoking that stuff a lot lately.'"

"We smoke normally in our house, but my son knows the difference between a regular cigarette and pot," Irma reported. "He doesn't associate it with any alteration in our behavior, but he'll come downstairs and tell me, 'Mommy, Daddy's upstairs making you one of those funny cigarettes.'"

"Does he ever ask for one?" Carol wondered. "My daughter asked me for one for show and tell. So my sister rolled her a joint with oregano and she brought it to school for show and tell."

"The teacher smoked it and thought it was the worst grass they ever had," Fred joked.

"Really." Carol slapped him. "She got up in front of her class for show and tell and said, 'This is what my parents smoke. My aunt rolled it for me.'"

"What were the reactions of the kids in school?" Sloman asked.

"Nothing." Carol shrugged. "Most of their parents smoke, so it didn't bother them."

"Would everybody feel comfortable with having a thirteen-year-old son or daughter who smoked?" Sloman asked the next logical question.

"Absolutely not," they all answered in unison.

"I think fifteen seems to be a good age," Fred compromised. "I don't think that junior high kids should be smoking grass. But for high school kids, it's okay. I have kids in my [dental] practice come in stoned. And kids tell me they smoke. In fact, I put appliances in a kid's mouth the other day and he said, 'Can I smoke?' and I said, 'It all depends what you're smoking.' I don't notice any degeneracy among them. I do amongst the pill takers. I do amongst the drinkers. And I have juvenile delinquents too. But the average nice kid that's smoking grass. . . ."

"That's great." Ira smiled. "They have their own roach holder. They just stick it between the wires."

Everyone howled. "I charge $400 extra for that," Fred deadpanned. . . .

Detrimental to Society?

"Do you think it's good from the point of view of the whole society that so many people smoke marijuana?" Sloman had directed the question to the orthodontist.

"Well, I'll tell you something," Fred started slowly. "I really have mixed feelings about it. I met a girl at a party. She lives in the same development we live in, and I really got to know her a bit afterwards. This girl is one of the most up people I've ever seen. So incredibly up that one day I said to her, 'Gail, how often do you smoke?' because it seemed to me that she was always up. She said, 'I don't smoke. I don't even smoke cigarettes.' I couldn't believe that. She was the most stoned-out-of-your-mind person I knew. So high on life. Such exuberance. But all the time. I thought she either had had a prefrontal lobotomy or was taking drugs. Nobody could be that happy all the time. That's the part of it that bothers me. Knowing there's another way.

"Everyone would like to go through life like this girl. Very few people can. In order to rid yourself of whatever your tensions are and really get into whatever you're doing, grass gives you the edge to get that high. So why not? Why not be that high? That high is a great spot. Unfortunately most of us need grass to get there. So from that point of view I don't think it's bad."

"I'm just amazed." Cusimano roused himself once again and stared bleary-eyed at the assemblage. "I'm really flabbergasted. I thought marijuana use would really decline. I thought it was a passé subject. You know most people have sort of gone beyond. I had no idea of this. God, it's really everywhere." He finished and sort of melted back into the couch.

"I think this is a very important thing to talk about," Barbara tried to raise the issue again. "Mary and I have discussed this before. I agree and sometimes I don't agree. Sometimes you tend to care less about things when you're stoned. Mary feels everything's going to degenerate and things won't get done. She feels society won't be productive. I, on the other hand, feel that what it probably does is it eliminates the anxiety over the idiotic things that go with getting things done, and the dumb things don't get done and the important things do. . . ."

"There's a name for what we're talking about." Soloman tried to steer them back to the subject. "It's called the 'amotivational syndrome.'"

Barbara looked impressed. "You mean it's a thing? See, Mary, we're getting an education."

"The idea is that if you smoke enough pot you're not going

to give a shit about anything," Sloman summarized.

"Ever?" Irma wished.

"It's true," Barbara looked upset. "Everything's crooked in my house. I laid everything on the table like an animal. You get sloppy. When we talk about productivity, are we talking about all the way from the top level down to the factory worker?"

"Everything. Factory workers, kids in school, the whole fabric of society." Sloman tried to talk over Irma and Steve, who seemed to have lost interest.

"We have to get serious," Barbara lectured them.

"We have to reach a consensus," Sloman continued. "This is a very heavy social issue. We're talking about social policy. We're talking about what sort of culture you want to live in."

"That's too heavy." Irma dismissed it with her hand. "I've had it with very serious. I want to laugh. Why do we have to conduct business now?" . . .

No Consensus Reached

"What's happening here is real endemic. This is where the issue divides," Sloman lectured. "There are people who want to smoke marijuana and think about how it's going to affect their lives, and there are people who want to giggle." He gave Irma a condescending look.

"Right." Mary was sweet in her earnestness. "I think about it too much. I do. I spend too much time thinking about what's happening to the children."

"I think that amotivational behavior certainly does enter into it," Fred admitted. "Which would mean that you would have to have some control. That doesn't mean that it couldn't be controlled."

"One of the first things said here tonight was, 'Boy, wouldn't it be great if for one day everyone in America smoked. What a peaceful place we would have.' I don't know if that's true," Sloman said ruefully. "I don't know."

"With so many people smoking grass today you don't read

articles about people smoking it and routinely jumping off the George Washington Bridge," Fred said. "It just doesn't happen. I have never met or witnessed anybody becoming hostile after smoking grass."

"But how many times have you smoked grass with someone who would resolve situations in a hostile manner even if they hadn't smoked grass? To whom hostility and aggression is a plausible reaction?" Sloman wondered.

"I don't smoke grass with the Hell's Angels," Fred shrugged.

"As a rule do you see a lot of middle-class people ever express themselves violently?" Sloman persisted.

"No," Fred admitted. "The people I would be with would never slug it out.". . .

Barbara looked mesmerized. "Did you shut off the tape recorder yet?" There was a plea in her voice.

"No, why?" Sloman asked.

"I wanted to know if it was party time yet," the young executive whined. Sensing defeat, Sloman relented. "Yeah, it's party time."

"Okay, gang," Barbara squealed with delight. "We got hot fudge and sprinkles on the table, the ice cream's beginning to melt; better dig in."

The Social Impact of Marijuana Use Among Youth

U.S. Commission on Marihuana and Drug Abuse

In the early 1970s, Congress created the U.S. Commission on Marihuana and Drug Abuse to study the scope and nature of marijuana use in the United States. The commission concluded that experimental and intermittent marijuana use was relatively harmless and advocated partial legalization of the drug. In the following selection excerpted from its final report, the commission evaluates the social effects of the increasing use of marijuana among young people. The authors conclude that this trend is not a threat to society. Although marijuana is used by youths who make up the counterculture, there is no evidence that marijuana is the cause of anti-establishment activities. Instead, the commission maintains, increased marijuana use is simply one of the many social changes to emerge from the tumultuous era of the 1960s.

For more than 30 years it has been widely assumed that the marihuana user constitutes a threat to the well-being of the community and the nation. Originally, the users were considered to be "outsiders" or marginal citizens. Included were such people as hustlers, prostitutes, itinerant workers, merchant seamen, miners and ranchhands, water-front day laborers and drifters, many of whom were drawn from the lower socioeconomic segments of the population.

U.S. Commission on Marihuana and Drug Abuse, *Marihuana: A Signal of Misunderstanding*. Washington, DC: U.S. Government Printing Office, 1972.

Concerns about marihuana use expressed in the 1930's related primarily to a perceived inconsistency between the life styles and values of these individuals and the social and moral order. Their potential influence on the young was especially worrisome. When marihuana was first prohibited, a recurrent fear was that use might spread among the youth. And in the late 1930's and 1940's, the attraction of young people to jazz music was thought to be in part related to marihuana use by this "outsider" population.

Throughout this early period, American society, in reaction to its fear of the unfamiliar, translated rumor about the criminality and immorality of the marihuana user into "unquestioned fact" which, in turn, was translated into social policy.

From the mid-thirties to the present, however, social perceptions have undergone significant change in response to the emergence of new and challenging social problems. As marihuana use has spread to include the affluent, middle class, white high school and college-age youth as well as minority group members of lower socioeconomic circumstances in urban core areas, the concept of marginality has become blurred.

Also, as the use of marihuana has increased, those individuals formerly labeled as marginal and threatening have been replaced by a more middle class, white, educated and younger population of marihuana smokers. A stereotyped user no longer exists, and therefore, the question now properly focuses on who poses a threat to the dominant order. . . .

The Young Marihuana User

The widespread use of marihuana by millions of young people of college and high school age has been viewed by many as a direct threat to the stability and future of the social order.

Many parents, adults in general, and government officials have expressed concern that young people who use marihuana often reject the essential values and traditions upon which the society is founded. Some have suggested that youthful mari-

huana use is, in itself, an indication of the rejection of responsibility and a sign of reckless hedonism which may well interfere with an orderly maturation process. Others see youthful
marihuana use as part of a pattern of conduct which produces
dropping out, underachievement and dependency.

In short, the mass character of youthful marihuana use has
been frequently interpreted as a rejection of the institutionalized
principles of law and a lack of concern for individual social responsibility, which threatens the social and political institutions.

Implicit in this view is the assumption that a young person
who uses marihuana in spite of the law cannot be expected to
assume an individually and socially responsible adult role. The
strength of this fear is drawn largely from the vocal and visible "counterculture" to which marihuana is often tied. Not surprisingly, the concerns posed by an alternate youthful life style
are extended to the drug itself.

Threats to the social order are often seen, for example, in
the character of youthful leisure time activities, such as atten-
dance at rock concerts, occasioned by the high mobility and
affluence of today's youth. They are also seen in the new
modes of speech and dress and in the seemingly casual manner of their day-to-day living. Equally troublesome for many,
however, is the idea of intentional intoxication for purposes of
recreation.

Adult Perceptions of Youths' Marihuana Use

Such conduct and the more casual attitude toward sexual relationships as well as participation in radical politics have provoked increasing concern throughout the adult society. The
National Survey [sponsored by the commission] illustrates the
extent to which the older adult perceives youthful marihuana
use as part of a much larger pattern of behavior which bodes
ill for the future of the nation.

First, the older the adult respondent, the more likely he was
to picture the marihuana user as leading an abnormal life.

Only 9% of the over-50 generation agreed with the statement that "most people who use marihuana lead a normal life." Nineteen percent of the 35-to-49 age group and 29% of the 26-to-34-year-olds were of the same belief. Conversely, half of the young adults (18-to-25) considered most marihuana users normal. This fact is not surprising since many of their contemporaries are marihuana users.

Second, the marihuana user, as envisioned by adults, is typically a youthful dropout from society. He doesn't like to be with other people, is uninterested in the world around him, is usually lazy and has an above-average number of personal problems.

Third, the less optimistic the adult respondent was about the nation's youth, the more likely he was to oppose alteration of the marihuana laws and to envision major social dislocations if the laws were changed. Fifty-seven percent of the adult population in general agreed with the statement, "if marihuana were legal, it would lead to teenagers becoming irresponsible and wild." Among those adults who most disapproved of youthful behavior in general, 74% agreed with the quoted statement. Similarly, 84% of the non-approving adults favored stricter laws on marihuana. . . .

Marihuana's symbolic role in a perceived generational conflict has brought marihuana use into the category of a social problem. Today's youthful marihuana user is seen as a greater threat to the social order than either the marginal user of earlier times or the adult user of the present. Since the concerns about marihuana today relate mostly to youth, the remainder of this section will focus on these youth-related issues.

The World of Youth

Youth of today are better fed, better housed, more mobile, more affluent, more schooled and probably more bored with their lives than any generation which has preceded them.

Adults have difficulty understanding why such privileged

young people should wish to offend by their language and appearance and spend so much effort trying to discredit those institutions of society which have made possible the privileges which those youth enjoy. Many adults perceive the present level of youthful discontent to be of a greater intensity than has been true of past generations.

Marihuana has become both a focus and a symbol of the generation gap and for many young people its use has become an expedient means of protest against adult values.

Adults in positions of authority, parents, teachers, policy officials, judges, and others often view marihuana use as the sign of youth's rejection of moral and social values and of the system of government under which they live. The problem is that both youth and adults tend to make pronouncements and are frequently unable to reason together in logical fashion. Instead they overstate their positions in such a way that effective resolution of their differences becomes very difficult.

In effect, each group takes the rhetoric of the other at face value. For youth, however, marihuana use plays many roles, only one of which is a symbolic assault on adult authority and values.

Marihuana Use as a Ritual

Marihuana use, for many young people, has become a part of a ritual. It takes on the aspect of participating in a shared experience which, for some if not all, is enjoyable in itself. For many, it becomes an even more interesting experience because it is forbidden.

Some of the rituals concerned with the purchase, storage, preparation, and use of marihuana take on a mystique similar to the time of Prohibition when people went through certain rituals necessary to get a drink in a speak-easy. The three knocks and "Joe sent me" cues have been replaced by the not-so-secret handshakes, the new vocabulary of youth and other exclusionary devices to delineate the "in" group.

The use of marihuana is attractive to many young people for the sense of group unity and participation which develops around the common use of the drug. This sense tends to be intensified by a sense of "common cause" in those circumstances where users are regarded as social or legal outcasts.

They know, too, that many of their peers who share the marihuana experience and also share the designation of lawbreaker are, in reality, productive and generally affirmative individuals who are interested neither in promoting the downfall of the nation nor in engaging in acts which would harm the general well-being of the community.

In short, many youth have found marihuana use to be a pleasurable and socially rewarding experience. They have found that the continuance of this behavior has brought them more pleasure than discomfort, more reward than punishment.

Rejecting Authority

Youth have increasingly come to see law enforcement activity directed at marihuana use as an unreasonable and unjustifiable rejection of their generation. Most of these youth have grown up with a positive image of the police as protectors of society. Now, many are confronted with the possibility of police intrusion into their private lives and the threat of a criminal record. The unfortunate result, in many instances, has been a blanket rejection and distrust of both the agents and institutions of government.

In part, marihuana use as a social behavior is an unintended byproduct of the formal and informal educational process. Some persons even suggest that youthful drug usage is a "success" in terms of the educational and socialization process. Our society values independence of thought, experimentation, and the empirical method, often reinforcing this attitude by such advertising cliches as "make up your own mind," "be your own man . . . judge for yourself."

Although experimentation with regard to drugs should not

be considered a "success," the Commission does believe that the educational efforts necessary to discourage this curiosity, which may be valuable in other matters, have not succeeded. We understand why teenagers and young adults encouraged over the years to make up their own minds have not been restrained by exaggerated accounts of marihuana's harmful effects, or by the more recent assertions that a true evaluation of marihuana uses requires more research. The Scottish verdict of "not proven" does little to restrain youthful curiosity. . . .

Most Users Are Responsible Citizens

We emphasized the difference between the vast majority of experimenters and intermittent users and the small group of moderate and heavy users who generally use drugs other than marihuana as well. The former do not differ significantly from non-users on many indices of social integration. Various studies indicate that they maintain normal patterns of living and social interaction, and are employed, competent citizens.

On the other hand, there undoubtedly are a number of persons who have used marihuana and have exercised poor judgment, performed inadequately, or behaved irresponsibly while under the drug's influence, thus jeopardizing themselves or others. The fact remains, however, that a certain number of these persons were immature and irresponsible individuals even prior to marihuana use, who would be expected to have poor or impaired judgment whether or not marihuana was involved.

The marihuana user is not, for the most part, a social isolationist or a severely disturbed individual in need of treatment or confinement. Most users, young or old, demonstrate an average or above-average degree of social functioning, academic achievement and job performance. Their general image of themselves and their society is not radically different from that of their non-marihuana-using peers. The majority of both groups tends to demonstrate equal interest in corporate concerns.

Based upon present evidence, it is unlikely that marihuana

users will become less socially responsible as a result of their marihuana use or that their patterns of behavior and values will change significantly.

Marihuana's Perceived Link to Social Problems

Society appears to be concerned about marihuana use primarily because of its perceived relationship to other social problems. . . . Here we consider the perceived impact of marihuana use upon the institutions and proclaimed goals of the society.

Many parents have a genuine fear that marihuana use leads to idleness and "dropping out." During the 1960's, marihuana use, as well as the use of other psychoactive drugs, became equated with unconventional youth life styles. When a number of young people adopted unconventional life styles, many adults tended to view long hair, unkempt appearance and drugs as symbols of counterculture.

They concluded that anyone who allowed his hair to grow or gave little attention to his clothing or appearance was probably a drug user with little or no motivation to achieve and no interest in conventional goals.

A number of researchers and clinicians have observed the use of marihuana or hashish in other societies, particularly among poor, lower class males. Some have observed that many of these individuals are generally unmotivated and ordinarily appear to show little aspiration or motivation to improve their way of life, regardless of whether they are judged by the standards of the more prosperous members of their own society or by middle class standards of contemporary American society.

One of the problems with this type of analysis is that it fails to perceive the social and cultural realities in which the phenomenon takes place. In the Middle East and in Asia where hashish is used, the societies, in all instances, are highly stratified with people in the lower classes having virtually no social or economic mobility. Poverty, deprivation and disease were the conditions into which these people were born and in which they remain, regardless of whether they use cannabis. In this context, a person's resignation to his status in life is not likely to be caused or greatly influenced by the effects of cannabis. Any society will always have a certain number of persons who, for various reasons, are not motivated to strive for personal

 THE HISTORY OF DRUGS

A Useful Area of Mind-Consciousness

Beat poet Allen Ginsberg was one of the many people who defended marijuana use in the 1960s.

How much there is to be revealed about marijuana in this decade in America for the general public! The actual experience of the smoked herb has been clouded by a fog of dirty language perpetrated by a crowd of fakers who have not had the experience and yet insist on downgrading it. The paradoxical key to this bizarre impasse of awareness is precisely that the marijuana consciousness is one that, ever so gently, shifts the center of attention *from* habitual shallow, purely verbal guidelines and repetitive secondhand ideological interpretations of experience to *more direct, slower, absorbing, occasionally microscopically minute engagement with sensing phenomena.*

A few people don't *like* the experience and report back to the language world that it's a drag. But the vast majority all over the world who have smoked the several breaths necessary to feel the effect, adjust to the strangely familiar sensation of Time slow-down, and explore this new space through natural curiosity, report that it's a useful area of mind-consciousness to be familiar with. Marijuana is a metaphysical herb less habituating than tobacco, whose smoke is no more disruptive than Insight.

Allen Ginsberg, "The Great Marijuana Hoax: First Manifesto to End the Bringdown," *Atlantic Monthly*, November 1966.

achievement or participate fully in the life of the community. Therefore, the determination is difficult to make whether cannabis use influences a person to drop out and, if it does, to what extent.

Marihuana Is Not the Cause

Some individuals possess particular personality as well as psychosocial characteristics which in specified instances could produce amotivation or dropping out. However, little likelihood exists that the introduction of a single element such as marihuana use would significantly change the basic personality and character structure of the individual to any degree. An individual is more likely to drop out when a number of circumstances have joined at a given point in his lifetime, producing pressures with which he has difficulty in coping. These pressures often coincide with situations involving painful or difficult judgments resulting from a need to adjust to the pressures of the social environment.

Many young people, particularly in the college population, are shielded in their earlier years from experiences which might be emotionally stressful or unpleasant. Some young people, so sheltered, are neither equipped to make mature and independent judgments nor prepared to enjoy the new-found freedom of the university or college in a mature and responsible way. Some of these students are often unable to cope with social or academic adversity. After being sheltered for so long, some of these young people may be easily attracted to experiences which promise new excitement and to fall under the influence of a peer group whose values and living patterns may be inimical to a productive, healthy and continuous process of personal growth and maturity. In these instances, marihuana serves as the medium by which these individuals encounter social and psychological experiences with which they are ill-equipped to cope.

Certain numbers of these young people have demonstrated

what is described as amotivation long before the smoking of marihuana became fashionable. Adolescence is often a particularly difficult period of searching in many directions at the same time. In addition to seeking a concept of "self" the adolescent is, at the same time, attempting to comprehend the nature of the world around him and to identify his status and role in society.

Different individuals, with different backgrounds, socialization patterns, belief systems and levels of emotional maturity cope with the period of transition from childhood to adulthood in different ways. For a small number, dropping out might be one of these coping mechanisms whether or not they use marihuana. For others, the response to the difficult adjustments of adolescence takes other forms, some of which are more acceptable, "normal" and easier for adults to understand.

The young person who does not find it possible to cope with the pressures of his adolescent developmental period in ways convenient to the understanding of adult society should not be rejected, stigmatized or labeled. He requires both support and understanding and the opportunity to participate in roles which have meaning for him and in ways in which he feels comfortable. For a certain number of young people, marihuana and the mystique of the experience eases this passage by helping them share their feelings, doubts, inadequacies and aspirations with peers with whom they feel safe and comfortable.

"Dropping Down"

Apart from the concern over youthful dropping out and idleness, there is also widespread concern about "dropping down" or underachieving.

Parents frequently express fear that marihuana will undermine or interfere with academic and vocational career development and achievement by focusing youthful interests on the drug and those associated with the drug subculture. Some parents make considerable sacrifices for their children to go to school, and the fears that marihuana might undermine the academic, emotional and vocational development of their young are quite understandable.

The Commission reviewed a number of studies related to marihuana use by high school and college youth. No conclusive evidence was found demonstrating that marihuana by itself is responsible for academic or vocational failure or "dropping down," although it could be one of many contributory reasons. Many studies reported that the majority of young people who have used marihuana received average or above-average grades in school.

In part, underachievement is related to a view of what one individual judges to be the achievement capacity of another. This judgment is often made without concern for what the individual himself feels about his potential, his interests and his goals. Perceptions about achievement also frequently fail to take into consideration the individual feelings about the goals of his peers and the values of the larger society, including the relative prestige and status attached to various academic programs, occupations and professions.

Youth and Radical Politics

Aside from the issue of unconventional life styles and the concerns evoked by them, the other major concern of the sixties which related to youth and drugs was radical politics.

During the latter half of the decade, youthful anti-war groups were organized on many of the nation's college campuses and high schools. These groups could be divided into two segments. The largest segment consisted of concerned, sometimes confused, frustrated and well-meaning petition signers and demonstrators. Within this large group there was a small coterie of individuals who constantly sought to turn the demonstration into a confrontation and to protest for peace by means of violence. The second segment consisted of organizations of individuals whose stated purpose was to undermine the social and political stability of the society through violent means.

What must be clearly understood, however, is that among the young people, and some not so young, who protested against the war in Vietnam, only a minority were bent on violence and manipulated and corrupted these otherwise peaceful demonstrations for their own purposes.

At the various gatherings, a number of the young people protesting in these mass groups did smoke marihuana. We will never know how many were initiated to marihuana use during the course of these peace demonstrations. The fact remains, however, that in the large campins, such as those in Washington, marihuana was involved in two ways. First, there was the "normal" use in which the smoking was part of the social experience. Individuals came together and smoked, in part, to acknowledge and strengthen group solidarity. Second, another quite different aspect of the marihuana use at these gatherings said, in effect, "we know it's illegal but go and arrest all of us for doing it. . . ." This aspect can perhaps best be characterized as a symbolic challenge to authority.

An Enemy of the United States?

Unfortunately, however, the media, particularly television and some of the news magazines, sometimes portrayed the image of a group of young people plotting the overthrow of the nation by violent means while under the influence of marihuana. In those relatively few instances where explosives and other violent means were employed, the evidence points to a cold and calculated plan which was neither conceived nor executed under the influence of marihuana.

As a result of these protests and demonstrations, therefore, radical politics has been seen by many as a mechanism through which large numbers of young people would be introduced to marihuana as well as to other drugs. Radical political activity or mass political protest is viewed by some as a threat to the welfare of the nation and is assumed to be aided and encouraged by our enemies.

The involvement of large numbers of youth in political activism and the concomitant public concern about drug use have beclouded the issue of marihuana use and have led to a broadening of the concerns about marihuana on the part of adults.

Some of the radical movement's leaders abetted this tendency by pointing out the alleged irrationality and unfairness of the marihuana laws to recruit members to their ranks. Not surprising is the fact that 45% of the adult respondents in the National Survey felt that marihuana is often promoted by people who are enemies of the United States. Nor is it surprising that this belief is a function of age. While 22% of all young people (12-to-17 years of age) and 26% of young adults (18-to-25 years) identified marihuana with national enemies, more than one-half (58%) of those persons 50 years and older did so.

Youth and the Work Ethic

Of the many issues related to youth and the use of marihuana, one that greatly troubles many adults is youthful attitudes toward work. The work ethic in our society is based on a belief that work is a good and necessary activity in and of itself.

The traditional view holds that work is not only a right and moral act but that it keeps people from mischief and from wasting time on harmful recreational pleasures. The rationale for this thesis is that work in American society has served as the primary means by which persons acquired the treasured symbols of society.

In fact, throughout much of our history, with the exception of the small number who inherited or married wealth, no ethical alternative to work existed. In recent years, the increased emphasis placed upon leisure time activities has resulted in shorter work weeks, longer vacation periods and more paid holidays.

Among the concerns of the adults about today's youthful attitudes toward work and leisure are that young people seem to enjoy their recreational pursuits so much that they forget that to a considerable degree their enjoyment is paid for by the labor of others.

Many young people do not express the same level of concern as their parents did about preparing themselves for a career and "getting ahead in the world." In part, this attitude is attributable to the fact that increasingly, the results of this labor are not tangible, material goods. Service occupations generally do not produce such tangible products, and even in manufacturing industries the individual worker is usually too remote from the product to feel any pride or interest in it. In both instances, the traditional symbol of the "manhood" of work, a tangible product, is no longer present.

In sum, society has become increasingly disturbed by certain attitudes of today's youth which seem to stress pleasure, fun and enjoyment without a counterbalancing concern for a disciplined and sustained work effort. Nevertheless, the number of young people who view work as unimportant is small when compared to the total number of young people. The Commission has found no evidence to suggest that the majority of youth are unwilling or incapable of productive and disciplined work performance. In fact, the great majority of young people are performing their tasks in industry, the professions and education quite effectively.

Although many young people delay entry into the work force to enjoy the fruits of our prosperous society, this delay does not mean they will not one day contribute their best efforts to the continued growth and advancement of the nation.

The Changing Social Scene

The present confusion about the effects of youthful marihuana use upon the dominant social order is caused by a variety of interrelated social concerns, many of them emotionally charged issues, including anti-war demonstrations, campus riots, hippie life styles, the rising incidence of crime and delin-

quency and the increased usage of all illicit drugs. The focus
of concern about marihuana is aggravated by the . . . out-
pouring of incidental information about the drug and its effects
in a form and volume far beyond the capacity of the readers or
listeners to assimilate or interpret. Rather than informing the
public, much of the data disseminated has produced frustra-
tion and misinterpretation of the information presented.

Adult society, including parents and policy-makers, finds it
difficult to comprehend and account for many of the attitudes
and behavior of the young, including the use of marihuana. In
many cases the adults are still influenced by the myths of an
earlier period which overstated the dangers of the drug. At a
time of great social change and turbulence, the tendency to
depend on the "traditional wisdom," and its moral justification, is a strong one.

Just as youth must try to understand and appreciate the
strengths of the institutions of our society, adults must try to
understand the times through the eyes of their children. Where
marihuana is concerned, society must try to understand its
role in the lives of those who use it. The key to such understanding lies in the changes which have taken place in society
within recent years and the effects these changes have had on
succeeding generations of youth. The increased use of marihuana is only one of these effects.

One focal point in discussion between generations is the
contrast between the use of marihuana and the use of alcohol.
Many young people perceive that marihuana is less dangerous
than alcohol in terms of its addiction potential and long-term
physical and psychological consequences. Many believe also
that marihuana—and other psychoactive drugs—make it possible to expand their perceptions and see this as a perfectly legitimate objective.

Viewed against the background of the profound changes of
recent years in the fields of economics, politics, religion, family life, housing patterns, civil rights, employment and recreation, the use of marihuana by the nation's youth must be

seen as a relatively minor change in social patterns of conduct and as more of a consequence of than a contributor to these major changes.

When the issue of marihuana use is placed in this context of society's larger concerns, marihuana does not emerge as a major issue or threat to the social order. Rather, it is most appropriately viewed as a part of the whole of society's concerns about the growth and development of its young people.

In view of the magnitude and nature of change which our society has experienced during the past 25 years, the thoughtful observer is not likely to attribute any of the major social problems resulting from this change to marihuana use. Similarly, it is unlikely that marihuana will affect the future strength, stability or vitality of our social and political institutions. The fundamental principles and values upon which the society rests are far too enduring to go up in the smoke of a marihuana cigarette.

CHAPTER FOUR

Current Issues
and Debates

The Pros and Cons of Marijuana Legalization

Part I: Alex Wodak, Craig Reinarman, and Peter D.A. Cohen; Part II: Colin Drummond

The following two-part article from the *British Medical Journal* provides both sides of the marijuana legalization debate. In Part I, Alex Wodak, Craig Reinarman, and Peter D.A. Cohen argue that the unjust punishments of marijuana users have created a devastating social divide between parents and children, doctors and patients, and police and their communities. They cite evidence that marijuana use and abuse are *not* more prevalent in countries where the drug is legal. Although they acknowledge that marijuana is not harmless, they argue that the social, economic, and moral consequences of its prohibition far outweigh the benefits. In the second half of the article, Colin Drummond argues that promarijuana lobbyists ignore the serious health risks of marijuana. For long-term users, marijuana smoking causes damage to the lungs and heart, impairs basic cognitive and motor functioning, and can exacerbate mental illness. Drummond does not believe that the British government would be able to successfully regulate a legalized marijuana market. Alex Wodak is the director of the Alcohol and Drug Service at St. Vincent's Hospital in Darlinghurst, Australia. Craig Reinarman is a professor of sociology at the University of California, Santa Cruz. Peter D.A. Cohen is the director of the Center for Drug Research at the

University of Amsterdam. Colin Drummond is part of the Department of Addictive Behavior and Psychological Medicine at St. George's Hospital in London, England.

Part I

Current debates on cannabis policy are dominated by attempts to establish the potential health costs of use of cannabis. While accurate assessment of the potential harms of cannabis is desirable, it is at least as important to estimate the costs—which are usually ignored—of current cannabis controls.

The Social Costs of Penalizing Marijuana

Perhaps doctors have often led the search for less harmful drug policies because the premier axiom of medicine is "first, do no harm." In 1893 Britain's Indian Hemp Drugs Commission concluded that excessive use of cannabis was uncommon and that moderate use produced practically no ill effects. In 1926, Sir Humphrey Rolleston, then president of the Royal College of Physicians, chaired a committee that recommended against criminalising opiates. Similarly, Dr WC Woodward, counsel to the American Medical Association, testified in Congress in 1937 to the lack of evidence justifying criminalisation of cannabis and several other commissions in Britain, Canada, and the United States have come to similar conclusions. In 1972, an American presidential commission concluded that marijuana "does not warrant" the harmful consequences of "criminal stigma and threat of incarceration." In 1978, President Carter told Congress that "penalties against the use of a drug should not be more damaging to an individual than the use of a drug itself; and where they are they should be changed. Nowhere is this more clear than in the laws against the possession of marijuana." Unfortunately, little has changed since President Carter uttered these words. The UK Police Foundation's review of cannabis policy in 2000 was the most recent senior international committee to reach the same verdict: "Our conclusion is that the present law on cannabis produces more harm than it prevents."

Beyond the substantial fiscal costs of enforcing the prohibition of cannabis, the social costs of such policies are considerable. Around the world each year, the lives, education, and careers of hundreds of thousands of people are damaged by the stigmatising experience of arrest. Families face lost incomes and emotional stress. Many cannabis users are already socially disadvantaged, so for them criminal penalties for possession of cannabis often entail additional costs, including disruption of relationships and loss of housing and employment. Current cannabis controls drive a wedge between parents and their children, health professionals and their patients, teachers and their students, and police and their communities. It is impossible for the many young people who use cannabis today to obtain reliable information about the concentration of psychoactive ingredients or the purity of samples they purchase, or even about less harmful ways of using the drug. Consequently, current cannabis policies are inimical to desirable public health outcomes.

Other serious costs are borne by communities. Despite its criminalisation, the use of cannabis has become so normalised that it is seen throughout most Western nations. Prohibition in the face of strong and consistent demand inevitably results in supplies being provided from illegal sources. The unregulated black market brings consumers of cannabis into direct contact with sellers of other illicit drugs. For example, in identical surveys of random samples of experienced marijuana users, 55% of respondents in San Francisco reported that they could buy other illicit drugs where they bought cannabis. In Amsterdam, where cannabis sales are regulated and rarely attract criminal sanctions, only 17% could get other illicit drugs from their source of cannabis. Allocating police to enforce the laws against cannabis reduces resources available to enforce laws against more serious crimes. The riches available in black markets increase the risk of serious corruption. During the last decade, royal commissions in two Australian jurisdictions concluded that police corruption was rampant and linked to drug prohibition.

Law Enforcement Backfires

The justification for cannabis prohibition is that it is supposed to reduce demand and supply, thereby reducing use and thus overall adverse health consequences. But demand, supply, and use have all varied widely over time, quite irrespective of controls. Evidence suggests that use is not increased by less intensive control. In the 11 American states that effectively decriminalised cannabis use in the 1970s, use has not risen beyond that experienced by comparable states in which it is prohibited. Similarly, the Netherlands for all intents and purposes decriminalised cannabis 25 years ago, but the prevalence there has remained roughly parallel to that in Germany and France and well below that in the United States.

There is an increasingly widespread view that international attempts to control cannabis by prohibiting its use have failed and cannot be remedied. Numerous professional associations in medicine, public health, law, and criminology have recognised this failure and the enormous collateral costs of prohibiting cannabis and have recommended consideration of less harmful regulatory alternatives. The Single Convention (1961), the treaty providing the major legal framework for international prohibition of cannabis, states that "a party [government] shall, if in its opinion the prevailing conditions in its country render it the most appropriate means of protecting the public health and welfare, prohibit [the use of cannabis]." Where is the compelling evidence that protection of public health and welfare is "most appropriately" served by the present laws on cannabis? Regulation of cannabis would not breach any nation's international treaty obligations. The major barriers to reconsideration of the punitive prohibition of cannabis are political, not scientific or legal.

All drugs have risks. Cannabis is not harmless, but adverse health consequences for the vast majority of users are modest, especially when compared with those of alcohol or tobacco. Attempts to restrict availability of cannabis by more intensive law enforcement have been expensive, ineffective, and usually counter productive. The belief that more intensive law enforcement will achieve better public health outcomes represents a triumph of hope over experience. If we discovered that a drug we had been using failed to relieve patients' symptoms and produced unpleasant side effects, would any of us increase the dose?

It is time to acknowledge that the social, economic, and moral costs of cannabis control far exceed the health costs of cannabis use. The search should begin for more effective means to reduce the harms that can result both from cannabis and from our attempts to control it.

Part II

Proponents of legalisation would have you believe that it is a harmless form of recreational pleasure. It is used mainly by responsible adults and the government has no place in interfering. Penalties for possession and use are disproportionate to the threat posed to the individual user or to society. Very few are harmed by its use: only a reckless minority gives responsible users a bad name by association. Besides, criminalisation fuels rather than prevents an illegal trade and fails to stamp out availability.

The above refers not to cannabis, but to handguns. The United Kingdom's already strict pre-1996 firearms laws did not protect the innocent from the 1996 Dunblane tragedy,[1] though on a wave of popular support from the media the UK

---

1. In 1996 Thomas Hamilton broke into a school in Dunblane, Scotland, and killed sixteen children and a teacher. He used four handguns in the attack.

government afterwards rapidly almost completely outlawed possession and use of handguns. Now the pro-cannabis legalisation lobby, supported by the same parts of the media that were outraged by Dunblane, seeks to legalise cannabis.

The pro-cannabis lobby conveniently overlooks the serious health effects of cannabis, pointing to its safety record in comparison with other illicit and legal drugs, such as tobacco and alcohol. The lobby would have us believe that cannabis never killed anyone. It is true that cannabis is relatively safe in overdose compared with heroin, but it is far from harmless in the longer term, particularly for heavy or regular users. The World Health Organization has concluded that cannabis, when smoked, is twice as carcinogenic as tobacco. It causes carcinoma of the lungs, larynx, mouth, and oesophagus as well as other chronic pulmonary diseases, with evidence of a dose-response relation. These carcinomas appear earlier than cancers that are purely the result of tobacco smoking. Cannabis increases the risk of death in people with heart disease. Furthermore, cannabis is now 10 times as pure as it was 20 years ago, which points to potentially greater health risks than earlier research has identified.

Psychological Implications

In vulnerable individuals, cannabis precipitates schizophrenia and other psychotic disorders and worsens their course. It is worth remembering that about 15% of schizophrenic patients commit suicide. This is not to mention other clear adverse psychological effects of cannabis, including depression, anxiety, and violent behaviour. Cannabis has up to 60 psychoactive ingredients, so it is hardly surprising that it is bad for the mental health of many vulnerable people.

Apart from death, cannabis also causes dependence in about 10% of users and in 50–90% of regular users. The number of cannabis users seeking specialist help has doubled in the past 10 years, accounting for 10% of attendances at drug treatment clinics in the United Kingdom. This is likely to be an underrepresentation, as most clinics tend to be geared more towards helping users of opiates. Also included among the risks are impairment of cognitive function, reduced academic achievement, teratogenic effects, immunosuppression, impaired fertility, and increased promiscuity and sexually transmitted diseases in regular users. As [J.] Henry has recently pointed out "it is perilous for the voice of science to be drowned out by campaigners for legalisation who are dismissive of the mounting evidence on dependence and harm."

The effect of cannabis intoxication on cognitive and motor functions is another aspect of the harm it does. Research on the adverse effects of cannabis in vehicle accidents is complicated by confounding factors such as alcohol intoxication, although in one UK study of fatal road accidents, no alcohol was detected in the bodies of 80% of people found positive for cannabis at necropsy. It is now recognised that the separate effects of alcohol and cannabis on psychomotor impairment and driving performance are approximately additive. And yet because of the absence of a roadside test equivalent to the breathalyser for alcohol, cannabis is much more difficult for the police to detect accurately. All of this points to appreciable social, health, and economic hazards of cannabis.

Other Arguments Against Legalising Marijuana

The pro-legalisation lobby claims potential benefits of legalisation in terms of curtailing the black market. But even in Holland, where cannabis has been quasi-decriminalised, some two thirds of the supply of cannabis takes place outside the regulated "coffee shop market." Further, with ⅛ ounce of cannabis costing on average as little as £5 in the United Kingdom, it would be difficult if not impossible for a legal, regulated, and taxed market to undercut the illegal drugs pushers. Just the same problems attend the growing illicit trade in "bootleg" alcohol and tobacco imported from mainland Europe to Britain, bypassing any regulation of sale, particularly of sale to vulnerable children.

Even the much vaunted advantages of cannabis for medical purposes have yet to be proved: so far the evidence suggests that cannabis has more adverse effects than do existing recognised treatments. If it does emerge that cannabinoids are efficacious in certain medical conditions, their licensing as medicines does not require any legal action and is a completely different matter from legalisation of recreational use of cannabis.

In any case, comparison with licit drugs such as tobacco and alcohol hardly provides a model for legalisation. Alcohol claims in excess of 40 000 lives a year in Britain and tobacco some 120 000. No similar estimate is available for cannabis, and no one knows what would be the final toll from its legalisation.

The cannabis "industry" is big business, accounting for a reported £4000m turnover a year. The recent share flotation of GM Pharmaceuticals, which manufactures cannabinoids for medical purposes, raised £25m and was six times oversubscribed. With legalisation, it would not be long before the discredited tobacco industry would find new markets for cannabis products. This same tobacco industry—which is roundly criticised for marketing a killer product and for its lack of ethics and its cynical exploitation of the vulnerability of the addicted public by concealment of the health risks—is hounded by the same press that now advocates legalisation of cannabis.

The pro-cannabis lobby would have us believe that a legal cannabis market could be successfully regulated by the UK government, when successive governments have for years failed to act decisively against the tobacco industry and are still failing to deal effectively with the alcohol industry. Two years on, we still await the government's response to Alcohol Concern's proposals for a national alcohol strategy.

A Threat to Public Health

The evidence base of the harms caused by cannabis is undoubtedly incomplete and the evidence in some cases is conflicting and confounded, but legalisation of cannabis would, on the basis of what we currently know, lead to increased use and increased harm to public health. As was the case with our old gun laws, no amount of regulation of a legal market would protect vulnerable individuals such as children and mentally ill people.

What we need instead is better public education on the true risks of cannabis and greater availability of treatment for people who are addicted. If there is to be any change in the law in relation to cannabis it should be in terms of the way the law is enforced, including greater consistency throughout the country, and a review of the penalties for possession, rather than any change in the statutes or any departure from international drug conventions. There should be greater emphasis on helping people experiencing problems with cannabis to obtain appropriate treatment.

Perhaps only a minority would be killed or injured by the legalisation of cannabis. But this would be of no comfort to you if your son or daughter was killed by a drug driver or sectioned into psychiatric hospital with a drug induced psychosis. The UK home secretary, David Blunkett, would be well advised to consider more fully the health risks of cannabis before proceeding with his decriminalisation proposal. Reducing police and court time through decriminalisation is likely to be at the expense of public health.

An Overview of the Medical Marijuana Question

Mitch Earleywine

From 1978 to 1992, the U.S. federal government approved programs in eight states that gave seriously ill patients access to
marijuana for the alleviation of their symptoms. In 1994, however, the federal appeals court upheld the decision by the U.S.
Drug Enforcement Administration (DEA) to refuse to reclassify
marijuana as a legal therapeutic drug. States responded by
taking the matter into their own hands; in 1996, California voters approved a medical marijuana referendum, and in 1998,
five other states followed suit. By 2001 thirty-two states allowed people to use marijuana for medical reasons despite the
fact that marijuana is still illegal under federal law. Because
states are not required to arrest people for federal offenses, the
federal Department of Justice (including the FBI and the DEA)
is responsible for enforcing its own laws. A medical marijuana
user in the state of California, for instance, would have to be
arrested by federal law enforcers and prosecuted in a federal
district court of California. In the following excerpt from his
2002 book exploring the latest scientific information on marijuana, Mitch Earleywine provides an overview of the questions
and concerns about medical marijuana. Although some evidence suggests that marijuana can help patients who suffer
from such diseases as glaucoma, AIDS, Parkinson's, and multiple sclerosis, much of the evidence is anecdotal and therefore

not conclusive. Earleywine believes that further scientific research is necessary. Mitch Earleywine is a professor of psychology at the University of Southern California. He specializes in marijuana research

Proponents of legalizing cannabis for medicinal use suggest the drug could help many who currently suffer from illness and disease. Opponents of the idea assert that the legal drugs currently available provide appropriate relief from relevant symptoms. These different viewpoints have inspired spirited debates. An unbiased assessment of the drug's costs and benefits requires extensive research. Investigations must reveal the drug's ability to alleviate symptoms without creating unsatisfactory side effects. This [selection] outlines a brief history of marijuana's medical uses and discusses important considerations in evaluating relevant research. An overview of marijuana's applications follows, examining the available data on its utility as a treatment for many physical ailments.

Smoked cannabis clearly helps some problems and may cost less than other medications. Synthetic cannabinoids can also alleviate symptoms of many disorders. Data suggest that cannabinoids can work well alone; they might also function effectively as part of a combination of therapies. For certain disorders, standard medications other than the cannabinoids remain the treatment of choice. Yet given the vast individual differences in reactions to medications, a few people may not improve with standard treatments and may respond better to medical cannabis. There is not enough research on most medical applications of cannabinoids to draw any firm conclusions about efficacy. Further work on marijuana's medical utility appears warranted.

The History of Medical Marijuana

Medicinal uses for cannabis date back to 2737 B.C., when the Chinese emperor and pharmacologist Shen Neng prescribed the drug for gout, malaria, beriberi, rheumatism, and memory problems. News of the medication spread throughout the world. The drug helped reduce symptoms in India, Africa, Greece, and Rome. Many authors assert that medical marijuana treatments would not have reached other countries unless they had meaningful efficacy. Dr. William O'Shaughnessy introduced the medication to Europe in the 1830s. By the early 1900s, some of the most prominent drug companies in Europe and America marketed cannabis extracts as cures for a variety of symptoms, including headache, nausea, cramps, and muscle spasms. Tinctures of cannabis may have had problems because of inconsistent potency, but they were often as good or better than other medications available for the same symptoms.

In the United States, the Marijuana Tax Act of 1937 discouraged medical (and recreational) use by requiring an expensive tax stamp and extensive paperwork. By 1942, against the recommendation of the American Medical Association, the U.S. Pharmacopoeia removed marijuana from its list of medications. This move eliminated research on the medical efficacy of the drug in this era, but recreational use increased. Users eventually noticed an impact on physical symptoms. Clinical lore about these medicinal effects spread. In 1970, the Comprehensive Drug Abuse Prevention and Control Act separated substances based on perceptions of their medical utility and liability for abuse. The act placed marijuana in Schedule I with heroin, mescaline, and LSD, making it unavailable for medical use. Despite this classification, the federal government allowed a few patients to receive the drug as part of a compassionate use program. Ideally, this program would have permitted data collection to help investigate therapeutic effects. New research on animals and humans eventually revealed medical potential for smoked marijuana, as well as individual cannabinoids.

By the early 1990s, the number of applications to the compassionate use program increased exponentially as people with AIDS sought relief from nausea and loss of appetite. The Department of Health and Human Services officially terminated the program in March 1992. Nevertheless, by the fall of 1996, California and Arizona had passed legislation permitting medicinal use of the drug. At least half of the remaining states have put forth comparable initiatives. These laws, however, conflict with federal legislation. Thus, possession of cannabis, even for medical purposes, remains a federal offense. Despite the risks, the rates of use for medical marijuana remain high. Research has continued, but only in very special circumstances, often using animals rather than human participants.

The Pros and Cons of Case Studies

Although research cannot resolve all the legal and ethical issues related to medicinal use of marijuana, it can address the drug's efficacy in treatment. Ideally, data on the utility of cannabis may inform these ethical and legal debates. Several key issues are important in evaluating research on medical marijuana. These concern the advantages and disadvantages of case studies and randomized clinical trials, as well as the relative costs and benefits of alternative medications. Case studies and randomized clinical trials each provide important information. Almost all medical uses of marijuana started with successful treatments of individual cases. One person found the drug helped alleviate a symptom and simply spread the news. Physicians published some of these reports, which occasionally inspired formal research projects. These case studies are superb for generating ideas for further work. Nevertheless, opinions vary on whether or not they provide enough information to encourage prescribing marijuana or cannabinoids. Fans of case studies emphasize that medical problems have unique features. Essentially, every use of every therapy is its own case study. Individual responses to drugs vary. As a result, physicians alter dosages and treatments based on ideographic reactions.

Proponents of case studies also mention that many medications gained widespread use based on only a few positive

results, including aspirin, insulin, and penicillin. They emphasize that large studies require considerable time and expense,
potentially preventing people from using a helpful drug. These
arguments in support of case studies can be particularly compelling when previous research has already established a medication's safety. For example, a few studies in the mid-1970s
showed that a daily aspirin might help prevent a second heart
attack. Yet a large study of the treatment did not appear until
1988. Without a large clinical trial, physicians did not recommend a daily aspirin to prevent a second heart attack. This
bias against smaller studies cost thousands of lives. Many
people died during the lag between the initial evidence and the
completion of a large clinical trial.

In contrast, single cases also have many drawbacks. People
tend to publish and remember the successful treatments but
forget the failures. Without a placebo control, we do not know
if improvements arose simply from expectation. Many symptoms ebb and flow with time. Perhaps some individual cases
would have spontaneously recovered without any treatment.
To minimize these potential problems, researchers perform
randomized clinical trials. They randomly assign large samples of participants to receive cannabinoids or a placebo. If the
treatment group improves more, the healing effects clearly do
not stem from some natural ebb and flow in the symptoms or
from a patient's expectations that the drug will work. These
studies are expensive and time consuming, but they can provide the best data possible. Clinical trials of many drugs receive funding from drug companies. Yet given the limited potential for smoked marijuana to generate a profit for these
companies, funding randomized control trials to establish its
medical efficacy remains difficult.

Costs Versus Benefits

Another issue important to the evaluation of medical marijuana
concerns relative costs and benefits. Many evaluators suggest

that cannabis must outperform all other available drugs in order to receive approval for treatment. Most supporters of this idea prefer established drugs based on the belief that they have lower potential for abuse. Physicians and patients must consider this cost relative to the drug's advantages. Critics of this idea accuse drug companies of interfering with marijuana research because of its low potential for increasing their profits. These critics highlight that the approval of other medications usually requires simple evidence of safety and efficacy, not superiority to other drugs. For example, the Food and Drug Administration (FDA) approved fluoxetine (Prozac) based on its ability to relieve depression better than a placebo. The FDA did not require data comparing it to other standard antidepressants. Thus, marijuana should only need evidence of efficacy

THE HISTORY OF DRUGS

A Call for Civil Disobedience

In the following excerpt, philosophy professor R. Eric Barnes argues that states should continue to legalize marijuana for medical purposes, despite the fact that federal law overrides state law.

At first it may seem that there is no point to state legalization [of marijuana], because the federal laws supersede state law. For example, it remains illegal to smoke marijuana for medicinal purposes in California, regardless of any law that the state may pass. States can remove their own laws against the use of medical marijuana, but nothing they do can make it legal—the federal government must act to make that happen. Nevertheless, there are two good reasons for states to pass these laws. The first is simply that, practically speaking, state law enforcement officials are less likely to aid in enforcing federal laws when their own state laws contradict federal law. So, passing these state laws may allow people to use marijuana for medicinal purposes without as significant a fear of prosecution. The second is that the states can effectively protest the obstructionist position of the federal govern-

and safety to receive approval for medical use.

In addition to established efficacy, the price of the drug and its side effects also contribute to its costs and benefits. Price and side effects play an important role in comparisons between oral THC [tetrahydrocannabinol], smoked marijuana, and other medications. Dronabinol (Marinol), the synthetic version of THC, costs as much as $13 for a 10 mg pill. (Typical treatments can require two of these pills per day.) The price of dronabinol can drop to approximately $8 for pills purchased in bulk. (A special program provides the drug to low-income patients at a reduced rate.) The same 10 mg of THC appears in half of a typical marijuana cigarette. This amount of cannabis costs less than $5 if purchased in bulk on the underground market. The price could fall markedly if the National Institute on Drug

ment by passing these laws. This form of protest is analogous in many respects to civil disobedience, and this makes an important contribution to justifying state legalization. . . .

The exact nature of civil disobedience is contentious, but many of the basic principles are generally agreed upon. The central features are that it be: an illegal act, a public act aimed at changing the law, and a conscientious political objection based on shared values. It can be easily shown that a state which legalized medical marijuana would be engaging in a public act that expresses a conscientious political objection based on shared values—and their goal should be a change in federal law. Setting aside that state legalization may not be illegal (strictly speaking), state legalization fits all of the criteria for being an act of civil disobedience. . . .

The states should take action that will motivate the federal government to change its stance on this issue, which it appears unwilling to do without provocation.

R. Eric Barnes, "Reefer Madness: Legal and Moral Issues Surrounding the Medical Prescription of Marijuana," *Bioethics*, vol. 14, January 2000, pp. 17–41.

Abuse (NIDA) provided the marijuana or if the government lifted legal sanctions. Thus, smoked marijuana is cheaper, providing a clear advantage over oral THC and many other drugs.

Smoked marijuana also may have fewer side effects than oral THC and many other drugs. Patients can smoke a small amount, notice effects in a few minutes, and alter their dosages to keep adverse reactions to a minimum. . . . Smoked marijuana for brief interventions or as a treatment for the terminally ill has no more negative side effects than many other popular drugs.

Controlled studies reveal that cannabinoids can decrease pressure inside the eye for glaucoma patients, alleviate pain, reduce vomiting, enhance appetite, promote weight gain, and minimize spasticity and involuntary movement. Other work suggests additional therapeutic effects for asthma, insomnia, and anxiety. Yet only a few studies have compared cannabinoids to established treatments for these problems. Case studies and animal research suggest that the drug may also help a host of other medical and psychological conditions. These include seizures, tumors, insomnia, menstrual cramps, premenstrual syndrome, Crohn's disease, tinnitus, schizophrenia, adult attention deficit disorder, uncontrollable violent episodes, post-traumatic stress disorder, and, surprisingly, drug addiction. The cases may provide enough evidence to stimulate researchers to conduct randomized clinical trials examining the impact of cannabinoids on these problems. . . .

Legal Considerations

A few states have passed legislation approving marijuana prescriptions for patients. Nevertheless, possession of cannabis still violates federal laws that carry penalties of fine, imprisonment, and forfeiture of property. These federal penalties apply even in states that have passed medical marijuana laws. Thus, local authorities may not prosecute medical marijuana users, but federal authorities often do. Legal advisors recommend that any attempts to obtain marijuana for medical purposes should follow legal channels first. A number of steps may help establish medicinal need, which may augment defense if a medical user is arrested. Treatments should begin with THC in pill form, obtained through a physician's prescription. Reactions to THC in this form may prove appropriately positive, eliminating the need to use marijuana. Any reactions to the drug should appear in medical records. If synthetic THC does not alleviate symptoms, patients should apply to the Investigational New Drug program through their physicians. Although the program remains closed, evidence of these attempts may help a later defense of medical necessity. Patients should implore appropriate state agencies and ask local politicians to appeal to programs on their behalf.

If none of these steps leads to permission, patients should carefully weigh the pros and cons of medical marijuana before violating federal laws. Patients who choose to use marijuana therapeutically should report it to their physician and monitor any changes in symptoms or decreases in other medications. Under no circumstances should the medicine be shared, sold, or given away. Patients should never grow or obtain more than an adequate supply for personal use. Given that many states increase penalties for possession of more than an ounce of cannabis, patients might consider always owning less than this amount. This decision to use medical marijuana can prove extremely risky. The complexities of this process reveal the odd and conflicted attitudes many Americans have about the medical use of this drug.

Additional Studies Are Necessary

The following list summarizes the efficacy of cannabinoid drugs for medical conditions:

Little evidence for efficacy
Huntington's
Parkinson's

Potential evidence for efficacy
anxiety
arthritis
dystonia
insomnia
microbes
seizures
Tourette's
tumors

Effective
appetite loss
glaucoma (alternative treatments may work better)
nausea and vomiting (alternative treatments may work
    better, but they cost more)
pain
spasticity
weight loss

Therapeutic use of marijuana and cannabinoids has a history spanning over 4,500 years. Research issues related to establishing the efficacy of medicinal cannabinoids remain complex. The costs and benefits of smoked marijuana or cannabinoids can vary widely, given the range of individual reactions to drugs. Medications that may work for the vast majority of patients can have little impact on others. These idiosyncratic reactions suggest that patients and physicians can only judge the utility of cannabinoids on an individual basis.

In general, cannabinoids show promise as medicine but require a great deal of additional study. Many patients report that smoked marijuana has advantages over oral THC. Smoking permits a quick assessment of reactions and an easy modification of dosage to minimize side effects. Yet given marijuana's current status as a Schedule I drug, researchers cannot investigate its medicinal properties. Most formal medical studies investigate dronabinol, the synthetic version of THC administered as a pill.

A few consistent findings appear in the literature on medical cannabinoids. THC clearly lowers intraocular pressure associated with glaucoma, but alternative medications function equally well. Smoked cannabis and THC can alleviate pain as effectively as established analgesics like codeine. Both smoked cannabis and oral THC can also lower nausea and vomiting. Other antiemetics may produce superior effects, but they often cost appreciably more. Both smoked marijuana and THC can enhance appetite in patients enduring chemotherapy or AIDS. (Smoked marijuana has some advantages over oral THC for increasing appetite.) These drugs help weight gain, too, though new, experimental medications may lead to greater increases in lean body mass.

Many case studies and a few controlled experiments suggest cannabinoids can decrease spasticity associated with spinal cord injury and multiple sclerosis. Evidence is less compelling for the treatment of other movement disorders, including Huntington's chorea and Parkinson's disease. Seizures may decrease in response to smoked marijuana or oral cannabidiol. Case studies support the medical use of cannabis for many other problems. Combination therapies that employ cannabinoids plus standard medications could have considerable potential, but researchers have not completed the appropriate studies.

Continued work on the medicinal uses of marijuana and the cannabinoids has the potential to enlighten us on the workings of the cannabinoid system. This research could also lead to improved treatments for many who suffer from numerous medical conditions.

European Laws on Marijuana Are Becoming Lenient

J.F.C. McAllister

In the following article published in 2001, J.F.C. McAllister describes an attitude of tolerance toward marijuana that has spread all across the continent of Europe. Holland was once the only haven for marijuana smokers, since adults can buy and smoke marijuana in the country's many popular "coffee shops." Now, however, European politicians outside Holland are beginning to respond to the public's shifting views and habits. Although an international convention in 1988 prohibited legalization of the drug, so many Europeans indulge in marijuana that European Union governments are opting for lax enforcement. In England, France, and Germany, police officers are now allowed to use discretion in deciding whether to arrest users and growers. The Spanish government does not prosecute users of *any* drug, so long as the use is private. In Portugal drug offenders are not criminals but patients; they are given the option of treatment instead of fines or incarceration. Not everyone in Europe supports this new, lenient drug enforcement; even in Holland 40 percent of people want to see "soft drugs" such as marijuana criminalized again. The United States also opposes legalizing marijuana. J.F.C. McAllister is a London-based correspondent for *Time* magazine.

Stroll down electric avenue in Brixton, south London, and three guys might offer to sell you marijuana within five minutes. It's

O.K.; the cops here won't arrest you for possessing a little. And it's no different on much of the Continent. Cedric, an 18-year-old Swiss student, smokes dope regularly with his friends on trains, in the streets and parks of Geneva, even during high school recess. "The teachers know about it but don't say anything," he says. In Marseilles two months ago, 20 crewmen on the aircraft carrier Foch had consumed cannabis so flagrantly on board that a military court had to punish them but handed out only suspended sentences. Judging by the fragrant smoke wafting around the ship, the crewmen estimated that two-thirds of their shipmates were equally guilty.

It used to be that Holland was Western Europe's only tokers' paradise, courtesy of 900 cannabis cafes where adults can legally buy five grams of marijuana or hashish. But now [2001], all over the Continent, the weed has won a new level of social acceptance. And where voters lead, politicians are following, as they ease up on criminality.

A European Union drug-monitoring report says at least 45 million of its citizens—18% of those ages 15 to 64—have tried marijuana at least once, and about 15 million have done so in the past 12 months. Young people toke the most: 25% of 15-to-16-year-olds and 40% of 18-year-olds have tried pot at least once. In the past decade, the number of people who admit to smoking at least once in the past year [2001] has doubled in many European countries.

When 45 million people have broken the law, the law may not be an ass but it is certainly an endangered species. Most countries still hang tough on hard drugs like cocaine and heroin, but when it comes to grass, they go with the flow. Despite lingering strict anticannabis laws—smoking a joint in Britain can technically result in five years in jail—the way millions flout those laws is pushing European governments to adapt.

Most are trying variants on what the Dutch call *gedogen*—turning a blind eye. The authorities keep marijuana-possession statutes on the books to conform with a 1988 international convention that prohibits outright legalization and to avoid the political controversy of changing the law. But they opt for quite lenient enforcement. Last month [July 2001] police in Brixton started a six-month experiment: they will caution users on the spot and confiscate their dope rather than book them for prosecution. The cops expect to save at least five hours of police work per nonarrest, which they will devote to street crime and drug dealers. In France and Germany, local police, prosecutors and judges are allowed considerable discretion to be tolerant. In Belgium the government proposes to make arrests only if marijuana use is "problematic" to the puffer or to others—so don't smoke in front of minors. Officials obviously expect few problems, since people will also be permitted to grow their own grass.

Some countries go even further. While dealers can still be arrested, Spain no longer prosecutes users of any recreational drug, including heroin, as long as they do it privately. In actual practice, it's common to see young people sharing a joint outside a club or even injecting drugs in a public square. Whether in spite of or because of the liberal regime, Spanish drug use has dropped over the past decade. Last month [July 2001] Portugal embarked on a similar decriminalization approach. First-time users of any drug are given suspended sentences; the hooked are deemed "patients," who are sent to a special drug-dependency board and offered treatment. If they refuse, they can be fined, sentenced to community service, blacklisted at discos—but not sent to jail. Carlos Rocha, spokesman for the Council of Ministers, says the old law simply "sent more and more persons to prison every year, and prisons became drug markets, drug-addiction nurseries."

Still, plenty of Europeans think decriminalizing marijuana is reefer madness. Even in Holland, 40% of those polled want the sale of soft drugs banned again, and 80% of localities bar the cannabis coffee shops. But advocates of coffee-shop sales think there's a major gain in isolating marijuana users—75% of whom are recreational dabblers, smoking once a week or less—from dealers who peddle harder drugs. "Separating these markets has resulted in less heroin use among young people," says Janhuib Blans from the Jellinek Center in Amsterdam. Today the average age of Dutch heroin addicts is rising steadily and has reached 40; a retirement home for junkies has even been opened. Peter Lilley, former deputy leader of the British Conservative Party, caused a stir recently by backing the sale of cannabis in licensed shops for off-premises consumption, just like liquor. The drug would, like booze, carry health warnings and be taxed. But unlike in Holland, it would be procured legally from licensed growers. He thinks this will hurt drug syndicates and help make dope "simply boring"—the same reasons advanced by Swiss officials for a new law permitting legal production of marijuana for purchase by Swiss residents.

European liberality is unlikely to make a dent in Washington, where President Bush has said drug legalization "would be a social catastrophe." Despite rising numbers of marijuana arrests, the U.S. remains wedded to strict prohibition. But Washington will have to watch out for hemp-scented clouds blowing from north of the border. The Canadian Bar Association, the Royal Canadian Mounted Police and the Canadian Association of Chiefs of Police all conditionally support decriminalizing the possession of small amounts of pot. So does Joe Clark, a former Prime Minister who is leader of the opposition Conservatives.

It's already a lucrative export: British Columbia's underground marijuana industry employs an estimated 150,000 people and earns some $4 billion a year, sending as much as 95% of the output to the U.S. A recent pot poll shows that 47% of Canadian voters back its legalization. One entrepreneur estimates that will happen in two years; he is already drawing up plans for a string of cafes along the 3,987-mile U.S. border, proffering high-quality weed to go, in vacuum-sealed bags.

Washington will squawk as loudly as it can if Ottawa comes anywhere close to legalizing the pot trade. But as Europe is learning, it may be easier to knock down rogue missiles than to beat back a consensus among allies and neighbors who think it is smarter to live with cannabis than to fight it.

Hemp Should Be Used in Place of Scarce Resources

Robert Deitch

Robert Deitch, a promarijuana activist based in Los Angeles, has written a comprehensive, critical history of the cannabis plant in America. In the following excerpt, he argues that the United States should once more cultivate hemp for its vast potential as an alternative resource. Hemp is a tall, fibrous variety of the cannabis plant that contains less than 1 percent of THC (tetrahydrocannabinol, the primary intoxicant in marijuana). Hemp can be used in the making of textiles, paper, clothing, plastics, and foodstuffs. Since the Marihuana Tax Act of 1937, the U.S. federal government has prohibited the domestic cultivation of hemp. Nevertheless, U.S. retailers and manufacturers import a great deal of hemp fiber, hemp seeds, and hempseed oil each year from over thirty nations that harvest the plant. From these raw materials, paper, clothing, and other products are made and sold in the United States. According to Deitch, hemp is the strongest natural fiber, and it can be grown quickly and inexpensively. It does not require pesticides, does not deplete the soil, and can be made into paper, textiles, and building materials that last much longer than those made from wood. Industries would no longer have to destroy the world's forests, says Deitch, if hemp were used for paper and packaging products. In addition, products currently made from petroleum and petrochemicals—including fuels, plastics, foams, lubricants, and lotions—could be made from hemp oil instead. Deitch believes that the United States would benefit environmentally and economically if its laws again allowed for the varied use of this dynamic raw material.

When the products we need and use every day are made from a limited, in fact dwindling, reservoir of natural resources, we inevitably drive up the cost of producing those goods. Instead, we should take advantage of the alternative resources available to us. Why squander cotton, wood, and petroleum (and their byproducts, like plastics and paper products), which are no longer quite so abundant or cheap? Why not bring back hemp?

Outlawing hemp forced everyone to focus on the development and utilization of petroleum, which led to an unwise dependence on trade relations with many parts of the world that we do not control. It has hastened the destruction of the forests, devastated the environment, and contributed to five decades of inflation. Fortunately, many of these problems can and will be resolved by reimplementing our cultivation and utilization of hemp.

A Waste of Natural Resources

Not only are we wasting our natural resources, we are undermining the ability of the planet to support its human population. The biggest waste of forest resources is their use for paper and packaging products—an area where hemp could be substituted quickly and easily.

Had it not been for the timber industry's effort at replanting, the US was on track to wipe out its forests by 2000 (according to the USDA's bulletin #404, in 1916!). Trees simply do not grow fast. It takes between five and twenty years to grow a tree and most paper products (newspapers, paper towels, toilet paper, cardboard boxes and other packaging) have a life expectancy of about 24 hours. Trees should be saved for building homes and furniture with a life expectancy of twenty, fifty, a hundred years or more.

Newspapers are just one example of how we are wasting our natural resources. Packaging is another. Merchandise is shipped in boxes packed inside bigger boxes, and the bigger the box on a supermarket shelf the more exposure that product gets, the better chance of it selling. And let's not forget all the paper that business uses: invoices, statements, letters and advertising. The paperless office was a pleasant fantasy, but there is no sign of it arriving anytime soon.

As the worldwide demand for wood byproducts grows exponentially, particularly in the last twenty years, the world's forests are being devastated. In addition, many large forests around the world are dying from the effects of acid rain caused in part by our extensive use of fossil fuels and petrochemicals. The forests are the lungs of the planet, and we need those trees to convert carbon dioxide into the oxygen—more than we need them for paper towels.

Such concerns apply to all kinds of packaging products. McDonald's started packaging hamburgers in styrofoam containers (derived from petroleum) instead of just wrapping them in paper in the mid-1970s. The price of gasoline was already through the roof due to the oil embargo, and the proliferation of new industrial uses for petrochemical products competing for the raw material hardly helped keep prices down. In early 1988 McDonald's discontinued the use of these foam containers, but even today hundreds of thousands of restaurants still use similar foam containers for take-out orders. The production of this type of foam also has been implicated in depleting the ozone in the atmosphere, which may be causing increases in melanoma (skin cancer) cases.

The Versatility of Hemp

Hemp can help. Hemp grows fast. The large-scale cultivation and utilization of hemp would enable us to cut down fewer trees and would increase the amount of vegetation on the planet—that would contribute to improving the quality of the air we breathe. Switching to hemp in place of various fossil fuel products could decrease air and water pollution and reduce the impact on the atmospheric ozone. Wood and petroleum can be conserved for uses that only they serve best; but it is possible to reduce their use significantly.

Unfortunately, we've paid little more than lip service to the idea of reducing our consumption of these resources, because the government has failed to develop alternatives to either petroleum or wood-based products. The government encourages recycling, but that is a waste of time and money as long as we continue to squander petroleum and wood resources on products with a short life expectancy. Although helpful, recycling is simply not a rational or practical solution to a problem of this scale—it is labor intensive and not cost effective. Resolving the problem lies at the point of manufacturing, which means developing environmentally safe and economically sound substitutes for the petroleum and wood-based products we currently produce and use. Hemp, Cannabis, is a fast-growing "renewable" resource that clearly makes sense as the basis for paper and various other products.

Until 1940, hemp-based products were the worldwide standard that everything else was judged against. Paper, cardboard, fabrics, plastics, fuel, building materials and lubricants of all kinds, products we use every day, could easily be made from hemp or hemp oil, and at a much lower cost than we currently pay. In fact, in many instances the quality of the products would go up. Hemp is one of the most versatile and fastest growing plants on the planet. Its long fibers are the strongest natural fiber known; yet it has also long been made into the world's finest cloth. Hemp-based paper lasts three times longer (225 years) than wood-based paper (75 years) and does not yellow. Hemp-based cardboard boxes are stronger than wood-based cardboard boxes. Even hemp-based building material (plywood sheeting and manufactured dimensional lumber) would produce homes that last longer and hold up to the weather better.

Hemp for Packaging and Building

The obvious starting point in re-implementing hemp as a viable resource would be the production of hemp-based paper, cardboard, and packaging products. We can produce four times the amount of paper pulp per acre from hemp than from trees, and we don't have to wait a minimum of five years for it to grow. Hemp grows to maturity in three or four months, and two (sometimes three) crops a year can be harvested off the same parcel of land, year after year. Hemp also does not require the highly toxic non-reusable and non-recyclable chemicals (sulfuric acid, to break down the organic glue called lignin and chlorine bleach to whiten the paper) that are needed to break down wood fibers into pulp, nor does it require chemical pesticides. (Because of the ever rising demand for paper products and despite environmental concerns, the US government currently allows paper mills to simply dump non-recyclable sulfuric acid into rivers and streams.)

Tree-free hemp paper, by contrast, can be made without sulfuric acid, chlorine bleach or any toxins, because the hurds (found inside the stalk of the plant) can be broken down with simple caustic soda, which can also be recycled. We already know how to use hemp for a wide range of paper and packaging products from toilet paper to cardboard and everything between. Hemp can be used to insulate homes, for wallpaper and for fiberboard for the construction. Books, documents, and artwork produced on hemp-based paper last three times longer and do not yellow. It is also stronger, and that is why, worldwide, paper money has always been made from hemp-based paper (a.k.a. rag bond—linen), including paper money in the US.

Hemp has also been developed already into a building material. Compressed Agricultural Fiber, CAF, is a sheeting material in the same genre as plywood, particle board, composite-board, and Masonite; it is strong, long lasting, termite free and less expensive. Because of hemp's long strands, it can be made into substitutes for laminated wood or composite beams. The construction industry is already using more and more composite materials, but these composite materials are still wood-based—either wood chips or sawdust mixed with a petroleum-based binding material. In fact, all of these composite materials can be made from hemp and hemp oil by-products, and they would not destroy the environment in the process. . . .

An Alternative to Flax

Most encyclopedias and dictionaries today describe "linen" as being made from Flax. Traditionally, fabrics made from hemp have also been known as linen. In fact, linen is made from several of the soft bast fibers—flax, hemp, and nettles, and mainly because of economic considerations often consisted of a combination of these fibers. It is practically impossible to identify whether a finished piece of linen fabric was made from flax or hemp. Actually, the majority of linen comes from hemp. Flax is unquestionably a more flexible fiber, even stronger, and is generally preferred for fine linens, but it is harder to grow and there are some strains of hemp, like Italian hemp, that are superior to flax for fine fabrics.

The important differences lie in the type and quality of the seeds and how the matured plants are retted. Retting (rotting) is the microbial decomposition of the stem of the plant, to release the fibers. This is accomplished either by leaving the mowed-down stems in the fields in the damp fall or by submerging them in water—water retting produces higher quality, lighter colored fibers.

Hemp yields about twice the fiber per acre as flax, but even more relevant is the fact that flax is "hard" on the soil, absorbing most of the nutrients, which is why it was not recommended to be grown more than once in ten years on the same parcel of land. That was not so important in colonial times when land was plentiful, but today it is. It also requires a good deal of attention and manual labor. Weed control is also a problem with flax and it is also susceptible to a variety of diseases, including races of wilt, canker, rust and blights. Hemp, on the other hand, is "good" for the soil and requires very little attention. Its deep penetrating roots break up and aerate the soil; it does not attract insects, chokes off weeds; and it can be grown on the same parcel of land over and over again. In many parts of the world hemp has been or was grown on the same parcel of land for well over a hundred years.

An Alternative to Cotton

Both flax and hemp fibers, with a tensile strength up to 80,000 pounds per square inch, are twice as strong as cotton. Textiles and cordage made from hemp fibers are much stronger and will last much longer than those made from cotton fibers. Furthermore, cotton crops are vulnerable to insects—and the boll weevil and his friends can only be eradicated with expensive and polluting petrochemical-based pesticides. The cultivation of cotton accounts for half of all the agricultural chemical pesticides used in this country. Hemp does not attract insects and does not require chemical pesticides.

Cotton no longer has the economic advantage of the cotton gin or slavery it once enjoyed, and although it has enjoyed almost 200 years of research and applied technology, today it is not cheap to produce compared to hemp. With a bit more research, existing hemp technology can be further developed to give us a wide range of hemp-based fabrics from delicate summer wear to the sturdiest of jeans, upholstery fabrics and carpeting. The original heavy-duty Levi pants were made for the California 49ers out of hempen sailcloth and rivets—the pockets wouldn't rip when filled with gold nuggets panned from the sediment.

The economic and environmental benefits would more than

compensate for the initial costs of re-tooling parts of the textile industry. All that is needed is to end the criminal sanctions against the use of Cannabis as a raw material.

Early Uses of Hemp as Fuel

As for petroleum, alternatives are already in the works. Ethanol, methanol and alcohol all burn substantially cleaner and cost less than petroleum. Late in World War II, the German army used alcohol to fuel its vehicles, including tanks. The US used methanol in the same period as fuel for bombers and jet fighter planes, and hemp oil was used to lubricate those engines. Today, most race cars and high performance cars run on methanol or pure alcohol and to improve air quality, several states have passed legislation that forces the big oil companies to include ethanol (made from corn stalks) in the gasoline they sell. Actually, both the combustion and diesel engines were originally designed to run on biomass fuels, derived from vegetation, not fossil fuel (petroleum). And hemp can provide that.

Henry Ford was operating a biomass cracking plant at Iron Mountain, Michigan, in the 1930s specifically to produce biomass fuel to run a fleet of automobiles. Hemp is by far the most efficient plant for such uses; it is the leading source of methanol (one acre of hemp will produce 20 barrels of fuel), ten times better than corn stalks—its nearest agricultural competitor. Cannabis is at least four times (possibly as much as fifty times) richer in biomass cellulose than its nearest rivals, corn stalks, sugarcane, kenaf, and trees. Petroleum is also being used to run our power plants (or worse yet—coal). Those generators can be operated on hemp-based charcoal or methanol; hemp contains no sulfur to pollute the environment. In fact, the Pyrolysis process used to convert fossil fuels into gasoline is exactly the same process employed in a biomass cracking plant.

Ford abandoned his Iron Mountain biomass cracking plant but in the short time that it was operating his researchers pro-

duced a number of chemicals commonly used by industry, ex-
plored various applications for hemp and hemp oil, and
demonstrated the versatility of Cannabis by producing an automobile made almost entirely of hemp—a picture of which
was published in 1941 in *Popular Mechanics Magazine.* The body
of the car was made of hemp-based molded plastic which was
ten times stronger than steel. The car itself weighed 1000
pounds less than a metal version, which means it could run
more miles per gallon. Even the fuel the car ran on was made
from hemp—meaning that operating costs were substantially
lower. Can you visualize an America where vehicles operate on
clean burning hemp-based methanol produced in the US, by
local workers? It is a practical, environmentally beneficial, economically responsible vision and moving in that direction will
dramatically reduce the US dependency on foreign-owned oil.

The "Perfect" Raw Material?

Practically everything that is currently made from petroleum
or petrochemicals could be made from hemp or hemp oil—all
kinds of plastic and foam packaging, lubricants, suntan oil,
toothpaste, shampoos and conditioners, all kinds of lotions,
and fuel for our cars and trucks—even the vehicles themselves.

Cannabis (hemp) is the perfect raw material. It is extraor-
dinarily versatile, its long fibers are exceptionally strong, it is
long lasting and environmentally safe, and it is one of the
fastest growing plants on the planet—growing as high as thirty
feet tall in three or four months. It is also very hardy; it does
not need groomed land or pesticides; it grows on any terrain—
mountains to swamps—and requires very little care. Cannabis
is even good for land and soil reclamation, as its long roots (up
to seven feet) aerate overworked soil. It breaks up compacted
soil while preventing erosion and mud slides, with the concomitant loss of watershed after heavy rain or forest fires.

The laws that have kept hemp illegal are artificially protecting the petroleum, petrochemical and forest industries. But

since Cannabis was outlawed in 1937, there have been dramatic changes. The petroleum companies no longer own the wells that produce the oil they are processing, so they are realizing much reduced profits. In addition, they are paying exorbitant transportation and exploration costs. And the supply is not infinite.

Because the cost of oil and gasoline keeps going up, the petroleum industry is on the verge of losing its primary market, the automobile industry. The search for alternative fuels and alternative technology (fuel cells and solar power) is progressing.

How Drugs Are Classified

The Controlled Substances Act of 1970 classified drugs into five different lists, or schedules, in order of decreasing potential for abuse. The decision to place a drug on a particular schedule is based mainly on the effects the drug has on the body, mind, and behavior. However, other factors are also considered. The schedule is used to help establish the penalties for someone using or selling illegal drugs. On the other hand, sometimes a potentially valuable drug for treating a disease can be incorrectly scheduled, greatly hampering the exploration of its usefulness as a treatment.

Schedule of Controlled Substances

RATING	EXAMPLE
SCHEDULE I A high potential for abuse; no currently accepted medical use in the United States; or no accepted safety for use in treatment under medical supervision.	• Heroin • LSD • Marijuana • Mescaline • MDMA (Ecstasy) • PCP
SCHEDULE II A high potential for abuse; currently accepted medical use with severe restrictions; abuse of the substance may lead to severe psychological or physical dependence.	• Opium and Opiates • Demerol • Codeine • Percodan • Methamphetamines • Cocaine • Amphetamines
SCHEDULE III A potential for abuse less than the substances listed in Schedules I and II; currently accepted medical use in the United States; abuse may lead to moderate or low physical dependence or high psychological dependence.	• Anabolic steroids • Hydrocodone • Certain barbiturates • Hallucinogenic substances

Schedule of Controlled Substances

RATING	EXAMPLE
SCHEDULE IV A low potential for abuse relative to the substances listed in Schedule III; currently accepted medical use in the United States; limited physical or psychological dependence relative to the substances listed in Schedule III.	• Barbiturates • Narcotics • Stimulants
SCHEDULE V A low potential for abuse relative to the substances listed in Schedule III; currently accepted medical use in the United States; limited physical or psychological dependence relative to the substances listed in Schedule IV.	• Compounds with limited codeine such as cough medicine

Facts About Marijuana

Delta-9-tetrahydrocannabinol (THC) is the chemical compound mainly responsible for the intoxicating effect of cannabis.

Hemp is a distinct and nonintoxicating form of cannabis grown for its fibrous stalks. Generally, it contains less than 1 percent THC.

Cannabis refers to marijuana and other drugs made from the same plant.

Cannabis sativa is an equatorial species of cannabis that does not grow well in northern latitudes.

Cannabis indica is a robust species of cannabis found mostly in the mountains of central Asia. It is shorter than sativa and has purplish green leaves. It is known as the more potent of the two species.

When left growing wild, cannabis can reach a height of five meters. It flowers naturally from late summer to mid-autumn.

Commercial-grade marijuana is a green, brown, or gray mixture of the dried, shredded leaves, stems, seeds, and flowers of the cannabis plant. It contains an average of 3 percent THC, and it is generally smoked in hand-rolled cigarettes (joints), cigars (blunts), pipes, or water pipes (bongs).

Sinsemilla is higher-quality marijuana because it contains only the leaves and buds of the unpollinated female plant; THC concentrations range from 7.5 to 24 percent.

Hashish refers to the cakes or slabs made from the sticky resin of the sinsemilla flowers. Its THC range is from 3.6 to 28 percent. Hash oil, a tarlike liquid distilled from hashish, ranges in THC content from 16 to 43 percent.

THC breaks up into eighty different by-products (or metabolites) before it is eliminated from the human body. Trace amounts of THC metabolites can linger in the blood, urine, and fatty tissues for weeks after any psychoactive effects of marijuana have worn off.

Some of the immediate physical effects of smoking marijuana are increased heartbeat and pulse rate, bloodshot eyes, dry mouth and throat, and increased appetite. Research also shows that marijuana affects the functioning of the short-term memory as well as the user's ability to learn and complete complex intellectual tasks.

Many factors can influence a person's psychological reaction to cannabis, including the concentration of THC in the cannabis, the user's mood prior to and during use, and other drugs or chemicals that may be present in the users's body.

Users of marijuana describe the psychological "high" as characterized by feelings of euphoria, giddiness, talkativeness, and tranquility as well as altered perceptions of time and space and fragmented ideas and memories. Users also claim a greater sensitivity in sensory perception.

The negative psychological effects of marijuana can include confusion, acute paranoia, anxiety, fear, and a sense of helplessness and loss of self-control.

Although a direct link to lung cancer has not been proven, many researchers believe marijuana smoke contains cancer-causing chemicals.

Although no one has proven that marijuana is physically addictive, research shows that many users can become psychologically dependent on the drug.

Marijuana is the most commonly used illegal drug in the United States. Approximately 80 million Americans admit to having tried marijuana at least once, and about 11 million admit to smoking it regularly.

In the United States there are more drug arrests for crimes involving marijuana than any other drug. Since 1993 there have been nearly 6.5 million marijuana-related arrests, 88 percent of which were for possession of the drug.

Cultivation of even one marijuana plant is a federal felony in the United States.

The use of marijuana for medical purposes is prohibited by federal law in the United States. Nevertheless, eight U.S. states have passed medical marijuana initiatives that allow seriously ill patients to have access to marijuana under state law. Those states are Alaska, Arizona, California, Colorado, Maine, Oregon, Nevada, and Washington. Patients who use marijuana in these states can still be prosecuted under federal law.

More than thirty industrialized nations grow hemp commercially, including England and Canada. Hemp is legally recognized as a commercial crop by the United National Convention on Narcotic Drugs, the North American Free Trade Agreement, and the General Agreement on Tariffs and Trade.

According to the United Nations, 141 million people around the world use marijuana.

CHRONOLOGY

B.C.

8000–4000
The Chinese use cannabis seeds for food and make textiles and clothing out of hemp.

2727
In Shen Nung's *Pen Ts'ao Ching*, the world's first medical text from China, cannabis is referred to as a superior medicine.

1400
Hindus in India record that the cannabis plant, or "sacred grass," is used for religious and medicinal purposes.

450
The Greek historian Herodotus records that for thousands of years the Scythians used cannabis for both practical and recreational purposes.

100
The Chinese are the first to make paper from hemp.

A.D.

800
The Muslim prophet Muhammad preaches that it is acceptable for his followers to use cannabis, but not alcohol.

1484
Pope Innocent VIII outlaws cannabis use as heretical and satanic.

1545
King Philip of Spain orders that hemp be grown throughout his entire empire.

1563
Queen Elizabeth I of England decrees that all owners of more than sixty acres of land must grow hemp or face a fine as punishment.

1619
Virginia makes hemp cultivation mandatory, and most other New World colonies follow suit.

1753
Cannabis sativa is classified by Carl Linnaeus.

1791
President Thomas Jefferson names hemp a necessity in the American economy; he insists that it be grown instead of tobacco.

1798
During his military expeditions, Napoléon Bonaparte discovers that hashish is smoked regularly by Egyptians; he prohibits his soldiers from partaking in the drug, but they bring the habit back with them to France.

1810–1812
Napoléon invades Russia primarily to gain control of the world's largest hemp industry.

1839
Dr. W.B. O'Shaughnessy introduces cannabis to Western science when he lauds it as an excellent analgesic.

1845
Jacques-Joseph Moreau founds the Club de Haschischins in Paris, where artists and intellectuals gather to experiment with hashish.

1850
A U.S. census counts 8,327 hemp plantations (at a minimum of two thousand acres each), growing cannabis for cloth and canvas. The *U.S. Pharmacopoeia* lists cannabis as a medicine for more than one hundred illnesses.

1868
The emir of Egypt declares that the possession of cannabis is a capital offense; Egypt becomes the first "modern" nation to outlaw cannabis.

1877
The sultan of Turkey makes cannabis illegal, with little effect.

1894
The Indian Hemp Drugs Commission issues an in-depth report about the use of marijuana in India and advises the British government against its prohibition.

1895
Pancho Villa's soldiers use the name *marijuana* to refer to their drug of choice; Americans quickly adopt the name into their popular culture but change the spelling to "marihuana."

1903
The first recorded marijuana smoking in the United States occurs in Brownsville, Texas, purportedly by Mexicans.

1911
South Africa bans cannabis.

1915–1927
Cannabis begins to be prohibited for nonmedical use in U.S. states, especially in the Southwest.

1928
The recreational use of cannabis becomes illegal in the United Kingdom.

1929
The U.S. government sponsors the Siler Commission's study of the effects of marijuana smoking by American servicemen in Panama; the commission recommends that no criminal penalties should result from off-duty use.

1930
Harry J. Anslinger is appointed head of the newly formed U.S. Federal Bureau of Narcotics and Dangerous Drugs (FBNDD); he holds the title for the next thirty-one years. Marijuana is at the forefront of his war on drugs.

1937
U.S. Congress passes the Marijuana Tax Act, which requires all those who deal in marijuana to register and pay a tax on it, and imposes heavy fines on those who fail to comply; this law paves the way for further federal regulations of marijuana.

1941
Cannabis is dropped from the approved list of drugs in the *U.S. Pharmacopoeia*. Henry Ford unveils a car that is made from, and runs on, hemp alone.

1942
After the Japanese invasion of the Philippines cuts off the supply of Manila hemp to the United States, the Department of Agriculture releases *Hemp for Victory*, a film urging farmers to grow hemp for the American war effort.

1944
New York City mayor Fiorello La Guardia releases a commissioned report stating that the marijuana problem in the city has been greatly exaggerated and that marijuana use does not directly lead to violence or crime.

1951
The U.S. Boggs Act, which calls for mandatory minimum sentences for violators of marijuana laws, is passed; it begins a chain reaction of "punitive legislation" throughout the United States.

1964
Dr. Raphael Mechoulam of the University of Tel Aviv discovers and isolates THC, the active chemical compound in marijuana.

1966
The Moroccan government attempts to purge the cannabis growers in the Rif Mountains.

1969
The British Wootton Report states that cannabis is not a particularly harmful drug.

1970
The United States passes the Controlled Substances Act, which lists cannabis as a Schedule I drug, on par with mescaline, LSD, and cocaine. Keith Stroup, an American lawyer, founds the National Organization for the Reform of Marijuana Laws (NORML).

1972
The National Commission on Marihuana and Drug Abuse (the Shafer Commission) states that there is little proven physical or psycholog-

ical damage from using cannabis; it also states that the legal punishment is out of proportion to the seriousness of the crime.

1973
The UN Convention of Psychotropic Substances declares marijuana to be a narcotic.

1975
The Mexican government begins spraying its marijuana crops with the pesticide paraquat at the urging of the United States, and the U.S. government begins cracking down on smugglers. The underground marijuana industry begins to move indoors in North America, where the art of the "homegrown" plant is perfected.

1976
In Holland, coffee shops and youth centers are now allowed to sell cannabis. Robert Randall, who suffers from glaucoma, is the first American to receive medical marijuana under the auspices of the U.S. government's Investigational New Drug Program. U.S. president Gerald Ford bans the medical research of cannabis.

1977
U.S. president Jimmy Carter calls for the decriminalization of small amounts of marijuana for personal use.

1983
Drug Abuse Resistance Education (DARE) is founded by Los Angeles police chief Daryl Gates; a nationwide antimarijuana campaign specifically targeted at youth begins.

1994
The U.S. Drug Enforcement Administration refuses to reclassify cannabis as a therapeutic drug.

1996
California passes a statewide people's initiative that legalizes medical marijuana within the state.

2001
The Canadian government passes legislation to allow patients compassionate access to cannabis.

ORGANIZATIONS TO CONTACT

The editors have compiled the following list of organizations concerned with the issues debated in this book. The descriptions are derived from materials provided by the organizations. All have publications or information available for interested readers. The list was compiled on the date of publication of the present volume; the information provided here may change. Be aware that many organizations take several weeks or longer to respond to inquiries, so allow as much time as possible.

American Civil Liberties Union (ACLU)
125 Broad St., 18th Fl., New York, NY 10004
(800) 567-ACLU
e-mail: aclu@aclu.org • Web site: www.aclu.org

The ACLU is a national organization that works to defend Americans' civil rights guaranteed by the U.S. Constitution. It provides legal defense, research, and education. The ACLU opposes the criminal prohibition of marijuana and the civil liberties violations that result from it.

American Council for Drug Education (ACDE)
164 W. Seventy-fourth St., New York, NY 10023
(800) 488-DRUG
e-mail: acde@phoenixhouse.org • Web site: www.acde.org

The American Council for Drug Education informs the public about the harmful effects of abusing drugs and alcohol. It gives the public access to scientifically based, compelling prevention programs and materials. The ACDE has resources for parents, youth, educators, prevention professionals, employers, health care professionals, and other concerned community members who are working to help America's youth avoid the dangers of drug and alcohol abuse.

Canadian Foundation for Drug Policy (CFDP)
70 MacDonald St., Ottawa, ON K2P 1H6 Canada
(613) 236-1027 • fax: (613) 238-2891
e-mail: eoscapel@fox.nstn.ca • Web site: www.cfdp.ca

Founded by several of Canada's leading drug policy specialists, the CFDP examines the objectives and consequences of Canada's drug laws and policies, including laws prohibiting marijuana. When necessary, the foundation recommends alternatives that it believes would make Canada's drug policies more effective and humane. The CFDP discusses drug policy issues with the Canadian government, media, and general public. It also disseminates educational materials and maintains a Web site.

Citizens United for the Rehabilitation of Errants (CURE)
PO Box 2310, National Capitol Station, Washington, DC 20013-2310
(202) 789-2126
Web site: www.curenational.org/new

CURE is a membership organization for prisoners, former prisoners, families of prisoners, and concerned citizens who want to reduce crime through the reformation of the criminal justice system. It emphasizes the need for rehabilitation rather than incarceration, especially where minor drug charges are involved. It works to establish awareness of these issues through conversations with the media and lawmakers. There are many state chapters of this organization.

Drug Enforcement Administration (DEA)
Mailstop: AXS 2401, Jefferson Davis Hwy., Alexandria, VA 22301
(202) 307-1000
Web site: www.usdoj.gov/dea

The DEA is the federal agency charged with enforcing the nation's drug laws. The agency concentrates on stopping the smuggling and distribution of narcotics in the United States and abroad. It publishes the *Drug Enforcement Magazine* three times a year.

Drug Policy Alliance
9250 Fifteenth St. NW, 2nd Fl., Washington, DC 20005
(202) 216-0035 • fax: (202) 216-0803
e-mail: dpf@dpf.org • Web site: www.dpf.org

The Drug Policy Alliance is an independent nonprofit organization that supports and publicizes alternatives to current U.S. policies on illegal drugs, including marijuana. The foundation's publications include the bimonthly *Drug Policy Letter* and the book *The Great Drug War*. It also distributes *Press Clips*, an annual compilation of newspaper articles on drug legalization issues, as well as legislative updates.

Drug Watch International (DWI)
PO Box 45218, Omaha, NE 68145-0218
(402) 384-9212
Web site: www.drugwatch.org

DWI is a volunteer nonprofit drug information organization that promotes drug-free cultures in the world and opposes the legalization of drugs. The organization upholds a comprehensive approach to drug issues involving prevention, education, intervention/treatment, and law enforcement/interdiction. It publishes a regular newsletter.

Lindesmith Center
400 W. Fifty-ninth St., New York, NY 10019
(212) 548-0695 • fax: (212) 548-4670
e-mail: lindesmith@sorosny.org • Web site: www.lindesmith.org

The Lindesmith Center is a policy research institute that seeks to broaden the debate on drug policy and related issues. The center houses a library and information center; organizes seminars and conferences; acts as a link between scholars, government, and the media; directs a grant program in Europe; and undertakes projects on drug policy topics.

Marijuana Policy Project (MPP)
PO Box 77492, Capitol Hill, Washington, DC 20013
(202) 462-5747 • fax: (202) 232-0442
e-mail: mpp@mpp.org • Web site: www.mpp.org

The MPP develops and promotes policies to minimize the harm associated with the consumption of marijuana and the laws prohibiting it. It seeks to make both medicinal and recreational marijuana legal on the federal level. To this end, the MPP researches the public health, economic, social, criminal justice, and other effects of marijuana consumption, and it works closely with Congress and other government bodies to implement humane marijuana policies. The project increases public awareness through speaking engagements, educational seminars, the mass media, and briefing papers.

National Institute on Drug Abuse (NIDA)
National Institutes of Health
6001 Executive Blvd., Room 5213, Bethesda, MD 20892-9561
(301) 443-1124
e-mail: information@lists.nida.nih.gov
Web site: www.nida.nih.gov

NIDA supports and conducts research on drug abuse to improve addiction prevention, treatment, and policy efforts. It publishes the bimonthly *NIDA Notes* newsletter, the periodic *NIDA Capsules* fact sheets, and a catalog of research reports and public education materials.

National Organization for the Reform of Marijuana Laws (NORML)
1600 K St. NW, Suite 501, Washington, DC 20006-2832
(202) 483-5500 • fax: (202) 483-0057
e-mail: norml@norml.org • Web site: www.norml.org

NORML fights to legalize marijuana and to help those who have been convicted and sentenced for possessing or selling marijuana. In addition to pamphlets and position papers, it publishes two newsletters: the *NORML Leaflet* and *Legislative Bulletin*.

Office of National Drug Control Policy (ONDCP)
Drug Policy Information Clearinghouse
PO Box 6000, Rockville, MD 20849-6000
(800) 666-3332 • fax: (301) 519-5212
e-mail: ondcp@ncjrs.org
Web site: www.whitehousedrugpolicy.gov

The ONDCP aims to reduce illicit drug use, manufacturing, and trafficking as well as drug-related violence, crime, and health consequences. The director of the ONDCP designs the National Drug Control Strategy, which steers the nation's antidrug efforts and establishes guidelines for cooperation among federal, state, and local government agencies. Drug policy studies are available upon request.

Partnership for a Drug-Free America
405 Lexington Ave., Suite 1601A, New York, NY 10174
(212) 922-1560 • fax: (212) 922-1570
Web site: www.drugfreeamerica.org

The Partnership for a Drug-Free America is a nonprofit organization that utilizes media communication to reduce the demand for illicit drugs in America. Best known for its national antidrug advertising campaign, the partnership works to "unsell" drugs to children and to prevent drug use among youth. It publishes the annual *Partnership Newsletter* as well as monthly press releases about current events with which the partnership is involved.

FOR FURTHER RESEARCH

Books

Ernest L. Abel, *A Marihuana Dictionary: Words, Terms, Events, and Persons Relating to Cannabis*. Westwood, CT: Greenwood, 1982.

———, *Marihuana: The First Twelve Thousand Years*. New York: Plenum, 1980.

Patrick Anderson, *High in America: The True Story Behind NORML and the Politics of Marijuana*. New York: Viking, 1981.

John A. Benson, Stanley J. Watson, and Janet E. Joy, eds., *Marijuana and Medicine: Assessment of the Science Base*. Washington, DC: National Academy, 1999.

Alan Bock, *Waiting to Inhale: The Politics of Medical Marijuana*. Santa Ana, CA: Seven Locks, 2000.

Richard J. Bonnie and Charles H. Whitebread II, *The Marihuana Conviction: A History of Marihuana Prohibition in the United States*. Charlottesville: University of Virginia Press, 1974.

Mark Bourrie, *Hemp: A Short History of a Most Misunderstood Plant and Its Uses and Abuses*. Buffalo, NY: Firefly, 2003.

Elizabeth Russell Connelly, *Through a Glass Darkly: The Psychological Effects of Marijuana and Hashish*. Philadelphia: Chelsea, 1999.

Sean Connolly, *Marijuana (Just the Facts)*. Chicago: Heinemann Library, 2002.

Robert Deitch, *Hemp—American History Revisited: The Plant with a Divided History*. New York: Algora, 2003.

Mitch Earleywine, *Understanding Marijuana: A New Look at the Scientific Evidence*. New York: Oxford University Press, 2002.

Patricia G. Erickson, *Cannabis Criminals: The Social Effects of Punishment on Drug Users*. Toronto: Addiction Research Foundation, 1980.

Jack Frazier, *The Great American Hemp Industry*. Peterstown, WV: Solar Age, 1991.

Charles M. Fuss Jr., *Sea of Grass: The Maritime Drug War, 1970–1990*. Annapolis, MD: Naval Institute Press, 1996.

Erich Goode, *The Marijuana Smokers*. New York: BasicBooks, 1970.

Lester Grinspoon, *Marihuana Reconsidered*. Cambridge, MA: Harvard University Press, 1971.

Lester Grinspoon and James Bakalar, *Marihuana, the Forbidden Medicine*. New Haven, CT: Yale University Press, 1993.

Ansley Hamid, *The Ganja Complex: Rastafari and Marijuana*. Lanham, MD: Lexington, 2002.

Jack Herer, *The Emperor Wears No Clothes*. Van Nuys, CA: HEMP, 1993.

Indian Hemp Drugs Commission, *Marijuana: Report of the Indian Hemp Drugs Commission, 1893–1894*. Silver Spring, MD: T. Jefferson, 1969.

Leslie L. Iversen, *The Science of Marijuana*. New York: Oxford University Press, 2000.

John Kaplan, *Marijuana: The New Prohibition*. New York: World, Pocket, 1970.

Andrew C. Kimmens, ed., *Tales of Hashish*. New York: William Morrow, 1977.

Fitz Hugh Ludlow, *The Hasheesh Eater: Being Passages from the Life of a Pythagorean*. New York: Harper and Brothers, 1857.

Alison Mack and Janet Joy, *Marijuana as Medicine: The Science Behind the Controversy*. Washington, DC: National Academy, 2000.

Patrick Matthews, *Cannabis Culture: A Journey Through Disputed Territory*. London: Bloomsbury, 1999.

Jacques Joseph Moreau, *Hashish and Mental Illness*. Ed. Hélène Peters and Gabriel G. Nahas. Trans. Gordon J. Barnett. New York: Raven, 1973.

Gabriel G. Nahas, *Keep Off the Grass: A Scientific Enquiry into the Biological Effects of Marijuana*. New York: Pergamon, 1979.

———, *Marihuana in Science and Medicine*. New York: Raven, 1984.

Michael Poole, *Romancing Mary Jane: A Year in the Life of a Failed Marijuana Grower*. Vancouver, BC: Greystone, 1998.

Brian Preston, *Pot Planet: Adventures in Global Marijuana Culture*. New York: Grove Atlantic, 2002.

Robert C. Randall and Alice M. O'Leary, *Marijuana Rx: The Patients' Fight for Medicinal Pot*. New York: Thunder's Mouth, 1999.

Rowan Robinson, *The Great Book of Hemp: The Complete Guide to the*

Environmental, Commercial, and Medicinal Uses of the World's Most Extraordinary Plant. Rochester, VT: Park Street, 1996.

Ed Rosenthal and Steve Kubby, *Why Marijuana Should Be Legal.* New York: Thunder's Mouth, 1996.

John W. Roulac, *Hemp Horizons: The Comeback of the World's Most Promising Plant.* White River Junction, VT: Chelsea Green, 1997.

Vera Rubin, ed., *Cannabis and Culture.* The Hague: Mouton, 1975.

Ethan Russo, Melanie Dreher, and Mary Lynn Mathre, eds., *Women and Cannabis: Medicine, Science, and Sociology.* New York: Haworth Integrative Healing, 2002.

Charles R. Schwenk and Susan L. Rhodes, *Marijuana and the Workplace: Interpreting Research on Complex Social Issues.* Westport, CT: Quorum, 1999.

Carol Sherman and Andrew Smith with Erik Tanner, *Highlights: An Illustrated History of Cannabis.* Berkeley, CA: Ten Speed, 1999.

Gary T. Silver, *The Dope Chronicles, 1850–1950.* New York: Harper Collins, 1979.

Larry "Ratso" Sloman, *Reefer Madness: The History of Marijuana in America.* New York: St. Martin's Griffin, 1998.

David Solomon, ed., *The Marihuana Papers.* New York: Signet, 1966.

Charles T. Tart, *On Being Stoned: A Psychological Study of Marijuana Intoxication.* Palo Alto, CA: Science and Behavior, 1971.

Robert P. Walton, *Marihuana: America's New Drug Problem.* Philadelphia: J.B. Lippincott, 1938.

Roger Warner, *Invisible Hand: The Marijuana Business.* New York: Beech Tree, 1986.

Lynn Zimmer and John P. Morgan, *Marijuana Myths, Marijuana Facts: A Review of the Scientific Evidence.* New York: Lindesmith Center, 1997.

Periodicals

Samuel Allentuck and Karl M. Bowman, "The Psychiatric Aspects of Marihuana Intoxication," *American Journal of Psychiatry*, vol. 99, September 1942.

Harry J. Anslinger, "Marijuana: Assassin of Youth," *American Magazine*, vol. 124, 1937.

W.D. Armstrong and J. Parascandola, "American Concern over Marijuana in the 1930s," *Pharmacy in History*, vol. 14, 1972.

Atlantic Monthly, "Reefer Dumbness," March 2004.

R. Eric Barnes, "Reefer Madness: Legal and Moral Issues Surrounding the Medical Prescription of Marijuana," *Bioethics*, vol. 14, January 2000.

Richard J. Bonnie and Charles H. Whitebread II, "The Forbidden Fruit and the Tree of Knowledge: An Inquiry into the Legal History of American Marijuana Prohibition," *Virginia Law Review*, vol. 56, 1970.

T.F. Brunner, "Marihuana in Ancient Greece and Rome? The Literary Evidence," *Bulletin of the History of Medicine*, vol. 47, 1973.

William F. Buckley Jr., "Who's the Judge of Medical Necessity?" *Los Angeles Times*, May 16, 2001.

Joseph Califano Jr., "The Grass Roots of Teen Drug Abuse," *Wall Street Journal*, March 26, 1999.

Albert E. Fossier, "The Marihuana Menace," *New Orleans Medical and Surgical Journal*, vol. 44, 1931.

Allen Ginsberg, "The Great Marijuana Hoax: First Manifesto to End the Bringdown," *Atlantic Monthly*, November 1966.

Ira Glasser, "Spotlight: Why Marijuana Law Reform Should Matter to You," *National ACLU Members' Bulletin*, Spring 1998.

H. Godwin, "The Ancient Cultivation of Hemp," *Antiquity*, vol. 41, 1967.

Leslie L. Iversen, "Marijuana: The Myths Are Hazardous to Your Health," *Cerebrum*, vol. 1, 1999.

Oriana Josseau Kalant, "Report of the Indian Hemp Drugs Commission, 1893–94: A Critical Review," *International Journal of the Addictions*, vol. 7, 1972.

Lancet, "Highs and Lows of Cannabis," January 31, 2004.

Richard Lowry, "Weed Whackers—the Anti-Marijuana Forces, and Why They're Wrong," *National Review*, August 20, 2001.

Jake MacDonald, "Joint Ventures," *Saturday Night*, April 1999.

J. Mandel, "Is Marijuana Law Enforcement Racist?" *Journal of Psychoactive Drugs*, vol. 20, 1988.

E. Marcovitz and H.J. Myers, "The Marijuana Addict in the Army," *War Medicine*, vol. 6, 1944.

J.F.C. McAllister, "Europe Goes to Pot," *Time*, vo. 158, August 20, 2001.

Jeanette McDougal, "Hemp, a Cover for Legalizing Pot," *Lexington Herald-Leader*, March 19, 2001.

Ethan A. Nadelmann, "Reefer Madness 1997: The New Bag of Scare Tactics," *Rolling Stone*, February 20, 1997.

New York Academy of Medicine, "Report on Drug Addiction," *Bulletin of the New York Academy of Medicine*, vol. 31, 1955.

Albert Parry, "The Menace of Marihuana," *American Mercury*, vol. 36, 1935.

Pamela Paul, "Marijuana Attitude Shift," *American Demographics*, June 2003.

J.R. Reynolds, "On the Therapeutic Use and Toxic Effects of *Cannabis Indica*," *Lancet*, vol. 1, 1890.

Hanna Rosin, "The Return of Pot," *New Republic*, February 17, 1997.

Eric Schlosser, "The Politics of Pot: A Government in Denial," *Rolling Stone*, March 4, 1999.

B. Spunt et al., "The Role of Marijuana in Homicide," *International Journal of the Addictions*, vol. 29, 1994.

Joel Stein et al., "The New Politics of Pot," *Time*, November 4, 2002.

Stuart Taylor Jr., "Medical Marijuana and the Folly of the Drug War," *National Journal*, May 19, 2001.

Tim Williams, "Medical Effects of Cannabis," *Pulse*, February 23, 2004.

Alex Wodak et al., "Cannabis Control: Costs Outweigh the Benefits," *British Medical Journal*, vol. 324, January 12, 2002.

INDEX

Dronabinol. *See* Marinol
Drug Enforcement Administration
(DEA), 141
drug trafficking, punitive legislation
has not suppressed, 78
Drummond, Colin, 132

Earleywine, Mitch, 141
Ebers Papyrus, 22
Egypt
ancient, use of hemp in, 22–23
crackdown on hashish in, 23–24
Napoléon's invasion of, 16, 35
Elizabeth I (queen of England), 28
England, use of hemp in, 27–28
ethnic minorities, association with
marijuana use, 88–89
Europe
early, hemp use in, 25–27
laws against marijuana are
becoming more lenient in,
152–55
nineteenth-century, marijuana use
in, 34–41

Federal Bureau of Narcotics, 80, 94
flax, hemp as alternative to, 161–62
Food and Drug Administration
(FDA), 146
Ford, Henry, 163
France, introduction of cannabis in,
37
free speech movement, 90–91
fuel, hemp as source of, 163–65

ganja, 35, 42
Gautier, Théophile, 37
Ginsberg, Allen, 122
Goethe, C.M., 59
Gonne, Maud, 40
government, U.S., conflict between
marijuana researchers and,
95–96, 143
Great Depression
repatriation of Mexicans during,
61
scapegoating of Mexicans during,
58–59
Greece, ancient
hemp use in, 24–25

marijuana use in, 66, 143

hashish, 16, 34
the Assassins and, 66
use of, by Sufi Muslims, 19, 23
Hashish Eater, The (Ludlow), 40
Health and Human Services,
Department of, 143
health risks, of marijuana, 137–38
Helmer, J., 60
hemp
advantages of, 158–60
as alternative to
cotton, 162–63
flax, 161–62
packaging/building material,
160–61
wood products, 157–58
commercial growing of, 13–14
as fuel, 163–65
plummet in use of, 41
use of
in ancient Rome, 25
in ancient world, 24–25
in early Europe, 25–27
in prehistoric China, 20–21
uses of, 12–13
Henry, J., 138
Henry VIII (king of England), 28
Hesychius, 24
Hiero II, 24
Holland
decriminalization of marijuana in,
135, 152, 153
hemp use in, 27–28
sale of marijuana in, 138
Hou-Han Shu, 21
Hsin Thang Shu, 21

India
use of hemp in, 21–22
uses of marijuana in, 30–33
Indian Hemp Drugs Commission
report, 133
summary of findings of, 42–50
Indian Hemp Tax, 35–36, 41

Jefferson, Thomas, 13
Johnson, Lee Otis, 99
Journal of the American Medical

alternative to, 160–61
paper, use of hemp as, 21
Payne Bill (1955), 80
Pershing, John "Black Jack," 56
Pharmacopoeia, 40
   removal of marijuana from, 89,
      143
"Poem of Hashish, The"
   (Baudelaire), 38
politics/politicization
   of marijuana, 94
   radical, among youthful users of
      marijuana, 125–27
Pollan, Michael, 12
polls. *See* surveys
Popular Mechanics Magazine, 164
psychedelic movement, 90
psychosis, marijuana's links with,
   were exaggerated, 44–46

racism, fueled fears of marijuana,
   52–61
Ramses III Papyrus, 22
Reinarman, Craig, 132
religion, use of cannabis in
   in Arab world, 23
   by Hindus, 21
research, federal government
   impedes, 95–96, 143
Reynolds, Sir Richard, 36
Rhymers Club, 40
Rimbaud, Arthur, 39
Robinson, Rowan, 19
Rocha, Carlos, 154
Rolleston, Humphrey, 133
Rome, ancient
   hemp use in, 25
   medicinal marijuana use in, 143

Saxons, use of hemp by, 26
Scythians, use of cannabis by, 13,
   16
Shen Neng, 142
Sherman, Carol, 34
Single Convention (1961), 135
Sloman, Larry "Ratso," 101
Smith, Andrew, 34
states, movement toward medical
   use of marijuana by, 144, 148
   argument for, 146–47

Stockberger, W.W., 57
Sufi Muslims, use of hashish by, 23
Supreme Court, on Marihuana Tax
   Act, 87–88
surveys
   on attitudes toward marijuana in
      Holland, 154
   on marijuana legalization in
      Canada, 155
   of marijuana users, 134
Symons, Arthur, 40

Tanner, Erik, 34
Taylor, Joseph F., 59
THC (delta-9-
   tetrahydrocannabinol), 12
   effects of, 14
   levels of, in hemp, 156
   synthesis of, 95
   synthetic form of, 15
      cost of, 147–48
tobacco, comparison to marijuana,
   75, 136, 139
Trembling of the Veil, The (Yeats), 40
Tulsa Tribune (newspaper), 60

United States
   banning of hemp cultivation in, 13
   early use of cannabis in, 39–40
   racism fueled fears of marijuana
      in, 52–61
U.S. Commission on Marihuana
   and Drug Abuse, 114
users, of marijuana
   accounts by, 103–13
      on parenting, 109–10
      on smoking habits, 106–107
      on starting use, 105–106
   change in, in 1960s, 89–90
   numbers of, 98
   public perception of, in 1960s, 87
   among youth, 115–16
      adult perceptions of, 116–17
      radical politics and, 125–27
      as rejection of authority, 119–20
      as ritual, 118–19

Venetians, hemp use by, 25
Victoria (queen of England), 14, 36
Vikings, hemp use by, 25

Villa, Pancho, 56

Wall Street Journal (newspaper), 98
Weil, Andrew, 95
Whitebread, Charles H., II, 87
Wodak, Alex, 132
wood products, hemp as alternative
  to, 157–58
Woodward, W.C., 133
work ethic
  counterculture and, 103
  youthful use of marijuana and,
    127–28

World Health Organization (WHO),
  95

Yeats, W.B., 40
Yolles, Stanley F., 98
youth
  education as best drug prevention
    tactic for, 83
  European, use of marijuana by,
    153
  marijuana use among, social
    impact of, 114–30